# Community Service and Participation Handbook

D1496774

(HOLT)

# Civics in Practice
## Principles of Government and Economics

**HOLT, RINEHART AND WINSTON**

A Harcourt Education Company

Orlando • **Austin** • New York • San Diego • London

ISBN 0-03-078004-7

4  5  6  7  8  9    912    11  10  9  8

# Contents

## Community Service and Participation Handbook

# Contents

## Community Service and Participation Handbook

Each chapter of the Student Edition has a Community Service and Participation Activity that provides students with the opportunity to gain firsthand experience with citizenship in action. These extended, multipart activities are designed for students to work individually or cooperatively. They ask students to meet specific learning objectives by examining some link between the chapter content and their own communities. Students apply the chapter content in the creation of a project that relates to one or more aspects of citizenship. The activities include planning, implementation, and assessment tools.

Included at the back of this handbook are a number of forms and documents that relate to chapter content—such as tax forms, job applications, and voter registration materials—for students to complete as practice for real-world experiences.

# What Does the Government Know About Your Community?

## OBJECTIVES

After completing this activity, students will be able to:

- Describe how their community looks and how the census gathers information.

- Compare the community's population in 1990 with that of the population in 2000.

- Explain why it is important to count each person in a community.

## OVERVIEW

In this activity, students will examine their community's participation in the 2000 census to determine how the population has changed since the 1990 census. Students will construct a chart comparing 1990 census information with findings from the 2000 census. The chart should clearly illustrate the changes in demographics, including race, economics, and family structures, as well as other information reflecting population changes.

## PLANNING

**Suggested Time** Plan to spend at least one 45-minute class period and one homework assignment on this activity.

**Resources** Students should be able to find census information in the library and via the Internet at www.census.gov. The 1990 census results are also available from this source.

**Preparation** Students should be able to calculate changes in the population statistics using the information they find.

## IMPLEMENTATION

1. Discuss the project with students. Begin by asking students to consider why the census is conducted every 10 years.

2. Distribute copies of the Planning Guidelines, Standards for Evaluating Work, and Task Sheet. Review these materials with the class and give students a time frame for completing their research and chart.

3. Once students understand the assignment, divide them into research teams. Students should access information from both censuses and do their comparisons. Students should focus on the demographics, including racial makeup of the community and economic conditions. On the Web site, have them click on your state from the pull-down menu, and then click on the county. The results of the 1990 census can be obtained by clicking on "browse more data facts" on the county page, and then clicking on the 1990 census information.

4. When groups have finished their research, they should create a chart. The chart should display the changes in demographics of the community.

5. Have groups present their charts and share information about the changes in demographics and economics in the community.

## ASSESSMENT

To evaluate students' work, use the Standards for Evaluating Work on page 3 of this booklet, along with Rubric 1: Acquiring Information and Rubric 7: Charts in the *Alternative Assessment Handbook* or in a customizable format on the One-Stop Planner.

## Planning Guidelines

In this activity, you will be working in a group to learn about the census and the population change in your community. You will be able to compare the 2000 census with the previous census conducted in 1990 to see how your community has changed and what populations have increased or decreased as a result. Use the library and other government resources to gather information about what the government learns from the census. Once you have gathered information, you should be able to compare how the population has changed based on population growth or decline in your community.

1. First, decide what categories you intend to include on your chart, such as race, age, family structure, economics, etc.

2. As you conduct your research, take thorough notes and keep a record of the sources you use. Discuss with your group which demographics you think should be included on your chart and why.

3. After you have completed your research, begin to organize the material for your chart. Remember to arrange the material so it shows the difference in population, including increases and decreases in the number of different types of people and families who have moved into your community since the last census.

4. Show your chart to the other members of the class. Compare your chart with the other charts created by your classmates and determine whether they discovered the same findings as you and if they listed the same demographics as your group.

5. Through this activity, you have learned that the government must count the population of each community to determine how to allocate valuable and limited government services.

## Standards for Evaluating Work

### EXCELLENT

- Research is complete and extensively explores the community's reliance on the census data. Sources are thoroughly documented and numerous. The demographics are accurate and provide ample information for the chart.

- Comparisons between the 1990 and 2000 censuses are numerous. Changes in demographics provided are well documented. The material for the chart is well organized.

- The chart produced is clear and well done. Information is easy to read and the comparisons make sense. The information is relevant and shows clearly the changes in demographics in the community.

### ACCEPTABLE

- Research is done with care and explores the community's demographics. There is documentation to support information for the chart.

- Comparisons between the 1990 and 2000 censuses are adequate. Resources allow for an average number of points of comparison. The material for the chart is organized.

- The chart produced is accurate and organized. Information is available and demographics are correlated.

### UNACCEPTABLE

- Research is poor and provides little information on the community's demographics. Sources are poorly documented.

- Comparisons between the 1990 and 2000 censuses are few. Resources do not provide adequate information for creating the chart. The material for the chart is non-existent or poorly organized.

- The chart produced is inaccurate and unorganized. The points of comparison do not make sense or are not presented well. Comparisons are not easy to recognize and the chart is not planned well enough to serve the purpose.

Name _____ Class _____ Date _____

## Task Sheet

Check off the following tasks as you complete the activity.

❑ **1.** Obtain a copy of the 1990 and 2000 censuses for your community. Conduct research that tells you what the demographics are in your community. Conduct research on these services.

❑ **2.** While you research, take careful notes and record the sources you use. Try to find interesting details to make your chart more useful and interesting.

❑ **3.** Before developing your chart, find other charts online, in books, or in magazines that compare data similar to the census. Notice how these charts are organized and present the material they are comparing. Organize your material so that it presents your comparisons well.

❑ **4.** Create your chart. Be sure to plot your points of comparison so the audience can clearly tell how the demographics provided have changed between the older census and the most recent census. Below your chart, describe the population so the reader can understand more about the demographics of the community.

❑ **5.** Show the chart to your class. Compare your chart to those created by the other groups. Discuss the importance of counting every person in your community so your community can receive its fair share of government services and resources.

# "And the Winner is..."

## OBJECTIVES

After completing this activity, students will be able to:

- Identify the senators from their state.

- Understand the job qualifications of a U.S. senator

- Describe the political process that results in a Senate election.

- Write a job description for a senator.

## OVERVIEW

In this activity, students will research the last senatorial election in their state. Students will discover what platform the senators ran on, who their political opponents were, and what the election results were. Students will be able to discuss the political process from the primaries to the final election. Students will research the office of senator as well as the background and record of their own senator to write a job description that describes the duties of a senator, both while in Washington, D.C., and in their own home state.

## PLANNING

**Suggested Time** Plan to spend at least two 45-minute class periods and two homework assignments on this activity.

**Resources** Students should be able to find information about their senators from the library. A senator's duties and qualifications should be available from the library or online. Information about the most recent election is available from newspaper sources as well as from the offices of the senators.

**Preparation** Students should be able to obtain information about their senators from press releases and the offices of the senators. Initially, you may want to divide the class into two sections and then into smaller groups for the assignments. The job description should be a collaborative effort between the two groups.

## IMPLEMENTATION

1. Discuss the project with the class. You might begin by asking students to consider first the U.S. Constitution's requirements for a senator. Other considerations or limitations on who may be a senator can be discussed. Then distribute copies of the Planning Guidelines, Standards for Evaluating Work, and Task Sheet to students. Review these materials with the class, giving students a time frame for completing their research and developing their job description.

2. Organize the class into two groups and assign the groups to research one of the two senators from their state. Then organize students into smaller groups for the research assignments.

3. Students should begin their research by first addressing the qualifications for running for office and then the election process. The political platform of each current senator should be described, and finally, the results of the election from the primaries to the final election should be noted. Each group can distribute the various tasks among its members, or the groups can break up into smaller groups for research purposes.

4. When groups have finished their research, have them develop a job description. The description should include not only the duties of the job, but the requirements for the job mandated by the U.S. Constitution, as well as characteristics desirable in a senator.

## ASSESSMENT

To evaluate students' work, use the Standards for Evaluating Work on page 17 of this booklet, along with Rubric 1: Acquiring Information, and Rubric 30: Research in the *Alternative Assessment Handbook* or in a customizable format on the One-Stop Planner.

# Planning Guidelines

In this activity, you will be working in a group to learn about how the two senators from your state are elected. You will first identify the U.S. senators who currently represent your state in Congress, and then research their election. In your research, you should determine who ran against them, what issues they focused on during their election (their platforms), and the results from the primary and final elections. Next, you should research the qualifications for becoming a senator, starting with the constitutional requirements. Determine what other qualifications, if any, are needed to run for this office and what qualifications your senators had for this job. Finally, you should write a job description for a U.S. senator, listing what you think the job entails. In other words, what do senators do every day in their jobs?

1. You should obtain the names of the two current U.S. senators representing your state in Congress. After identifying them, contact one of their home offices, usually located in your state's capital, for information about their qualifications.

2. After your group has been assigned a senator, conduct research on the last election. Gather information concerning the issues addressed during the election and the results of the primary and any run-off elections. Obtain the final election results.

3. Research the background of the senators. Find out what qualified them to run and what they did before becoming senators. Research what the duties are for a senator.

4. Write a job description for the job of senator. Be sure to include the duties of this official while in Washington, D.C., and while serving in the home state.

5. Through this activity you will learn that the election process often forces people with worthy attributes to compete against each other for office. You will also learn that it is important to identify issues that are of concern to the people senators are elected to represent.

# Standards for Evaluating Work

## EXCELLENT

- Research is complete and the student uses many sources for compiling the information about the requirements to run for election and the qualifications of their own senator. The data is accurate and contains information that will assist in creating the job description.

- The election results are complete and the background of the senator is well researched and documented. The job of a senator is researched well enough to create an accurate job description.

- The job description produced is cogent and logically presented. The job description covers the senator's duties both in Washington, D.C., and in the home state. It contains an accurate and full representation of what is required from a senator.

## ACCEPTABLE

- Research is carefully done and explores the election process and the senator's qualifications. There is documentation to support information for the job description.

- The election results are partially complete and show general information about the senator. The material for the job description is limited.

- The job description is adequate. The job is described in generic terms and does not contain information about differences in the job based on location. The job description shows some understanding of the functions of a senator.

## UNACCEPTABLE

- Research is poor and provides little information on the election process generally, or as it relates to this senator. Sources are poorly documented.

- The election results are inaccurate or incomplete. Resources do not provide information useful for creating the job description. The material for the job description is non-existent or poorly organized.

- The job description is inaccurate and contains little information about what the job entails. The job description shows little understanding of the functions of a senator.

Name _____ Class _____ Date _____


# Task Sheet

Check off the following tasks as you complete the activity:

❏ **1.** Obtain the names of the U.S. senators who represent your state. Conduct research on the qualifications of these senators.

❏ **2.** While you research, take careful notes and record the sources you use. Try to find interesting details about the job of a senator to help you in writing your job description.

❏ **3.** Before developing the job description, be sure to find out what U.S. senators do both in Washington, D.C., while working in Congress, and while working at home in your state. Organize your material so you can use it in writing the job description.

❏ **4.** Create the job description. Be sure to describe the duties of a U.S. senator while in Washington, D.C., and while serving in the state.

❏ **5.** Participate in a class discussion about the importance of making sure there are qualified people in the senate who can manage the country. Discuss some of the important qualifications of elected officials and why you think the U.S. Constitution requires what it does for election to the Senate. Discuss how the people benefit when they elect good and competent senators and other political representatives.

# The Equal Rights Amendment

## OBJECTIVES

After completing this activity, students will be able to:

- Trace the path of the Equal Rights Amendment (ERA) from its proposal to its defeat.

- Describe how an amendment to the U.S. Constitution is proposed.

- Debate the pros and cons of the ERA.

## OVERVIEW

In this activity, students will research the proposed but failed Equal Rights Amendment to the U.S. Constitution. They will learn how an amendment is proposed and what it takes to get a proposed amendment ratified. Students will also learn about the 10-year journey of the ERA, from its passage by Congress to its ultimate death by non-ratification. Students will be able to contact local groups that supported or opposed the ERA and will use the information gathered to debate this issue. Students should also become familiar with the prominent people who framed this legislation and the debate surrounding it.

## PLANNING

**Suggested Time** Plan to spend at least three 45-minute class periods and three homework assignments on this activity.

**Resources** Students should be able to find information about this amendment from the library and online sources. Students also can find magazine and newspaper articles on the issue. Many resources highlight the prominent figures representing the opposing sides in this issue.

**Preparation** Students should first discuss the mechanics of amending the U.S. Constitution. Then students should examine this amendment to discover how it was proposed. Students should contact organizations that participated in this debate.

## IMPLEMENTATION

1. Discuss the chapter with students, highlighting the section on amending the U.S. Constitution. Discuss the historical context of the Equal Rights Amendment. Distribute copies of the Planning Guidelines, Standards for Evaluating Work, and Task Sheet. Give students a time frame for finishing the research and set a date for the debate.

2. Once students understand the assignment, organize them into teams. Assign the teams either at random, according to sex, or according to their support/opposition to the amendment. Students can be organized into smaller groups to do research and plan the debate.

3. The research should first determine how an amendment gets proposed and what it takes to get it passed. Then students should focus on this amendment and its path through the process. Research should include determining the pros and cons of the amendment according to different groups in the debate.

4. When groups have finished their research, have them develop the debate. Arguments should be developed around the issues that the amendment was trying to address as well as the pros and cons of having women's rights protected by the U.S. Constitution. A debate can take the form of two individuals appointed to argue each side, or it can be a forum, with a panel of students selected to present different arguments within each issue in a point/counterpoint fashion.

## ASSESSMENT

To evaluate students' work, use the Standards for Evaluating Work on page 11 of this booklet, along with Rubric 10: Debates and Rubric 16: Judging Information, in the *Alternative Assessment Handbook* or in a customizable format on the One-Stop Planner.

# Planning Guidelines

In this activity, you will be working in a group to learn how the U.S. Constitution is amended and the process a proposed amendment has to go through to be ratified and actually become part of the Constitution. You will also follow the Equal Rights Amendment (ERA) from its proposal through its non-ratification—a 10-year process—to familiarize yourself with that process. In addition, you will learn about the ERA and what it tried to accomplish, and you will research the issues surrounding it. From your research, you will be able to describe the arguments used to support the amendment and those that defeated it. Finally, you will use the information you gathered to develop and hold a debate that expresses the same arguments made during the 10 years the amendment was debated in Congress and the state legislatures. Pay attention to the relevance of those arguments today.

1. You should research how the U.S. Constitution is amended. Also, determine how an amendment gets placed before Congress for consideration and what needs to happen for it to become law.

2. Research the ERA specifically to see how that amendment came before Congress. Trace the path of the amendment through its 10-year history from proposal to defeat.

3. Research the issues and how they were addressed by the amendment. Discover the main arguments for proposing it and the main arguments against its ratification. Notice who the main proponents were and who came to be the spokespersons for and against the ERA. Contact local agencies that expressed an opinion either for or against its passage and examine their position for potential arguments.

4. Write down what you think are the arguments for and against your side. Formulate a debate that supports your side of the issue. Remember to address what you think the other side is going to argue. If you are going to debate with only one person, choose that person. If you are going to present your views as part of a panel, determine who will represent the issues on your panel and help those students to prepare for questions from the class. Choose a moderator for the panel discussion.

5. Through this activity, you will learn the process of amending the U.S. Constitution. You will also learn how some issues divide this country, and how after all the issues are heard and all the votes counted, everyone, winners and losers alike, move forward to address the next issue.

# Standards for Evaluating Work

## EXCELLENT

- Research is complete and the student uses many sources for compiling information about the process of amending the Constitution. The student has also thoroughly researched the path of the ERA and has documented how this amendment was proposed and ultimately defeated.

- The student has thoroughly documented the arguments offered at the time the amendment made its way through the process. Issues that became the focal point of the debate are identified.

- The debate or forum has been persuasively presented and the issues clearly articulated. The student has found the main reason for and against the point he or she has argued. The debate or forum was well prepared, organized, and presented.

## ACCEPTABLE

- Research includes sources that provide information about how to amend the Constitution and information about the process undertaken for the ERA.

- The student has identified substantial arguments that can be used to formulate the issues raised at the time.

- The debate or forum has been organized and presented in a cogent fashion. The student has offered sound reasons for supporting his or her argument.

## UNACCEPTABLE

- Research is poor and does not accurately reflect the process for amending the U.S. Constitution. The ERA has not been accurately documented.

- The student has few arguments in support of his or her position on the issues.

- The debate or forum is unorganized and the student does not present the issues in a way that is persuasive or understandable.

## Task Sheet

Check off the following tasks as you complete the activity.

❑ **1.** Determine the process necessary to propose and pass an amendment to the U.S. Constitution.

❑ **2.** Research the ERA and determine the path it took through the ratification process. Pay special attention to dates and actions that Congress took to ensure its passage.

❑ **3.** List the main arguments used to support/defeat the amendment. Determine which groups or organizations made which arguments. Contact these organizations in your area to see what their position and involvement was in the support or opposition of this amendment.

❑ **4.** Determine who the main proponents and opponents were of the ERA. What were their main tactics when making their arguments?

❑ **5.** Determine whether you will present the issues in a debate or forum for your class. If a debate is used, choose the debater(s). If a forum is used, decide who will present which issues and who will respond to them. Choose a forum moderator.

❑ **6.** Have a class debate or forum. Present the arguments for your issue and counter the arguments used against your side. If a forum is used, present the issues in a point-counterpoint session so that each issue presented by your side is countered by a student representing the issue from the other side.

# Know Your Rights

## OBJECTIVES

After completing this activity, students will be able to:

- Describe the differences between their rights under the U.S. Constitution and their state's constitution.

- Describe the structure of their state's constitution and the amendments.

- Understand that the state's constitution addresses issues different from the U.S. Constitution.

- Understand how the differences between the U.S. and state constitutions affect the lives of citizens in their state.

## OVERVIEW

In this activity, students will research their state constitution. They will compare the Bill of Rights under the U.S. Constitution with the same rights in their state constitution to determine whether the state gives citizens additional protection. You may want to review your state's constitution and select some sections for students to use. Students will then write a *Know Your Rights* pamphlet for distribution to new citizens of their state. This pamphlet should describe some circumstances under which citizens have greater or different rights under the state constitution than under the U.S. Constitution.

## PLANNING

**Suggested Time** Plan to spend at least two 45-minute class periods and three homework assignments on this activity.

**Resources** Students should begin their research by obtaining copies of the state constitution, identifying the amendments to it, and researching their meaning. These sources are available on the Internet or in the public library.

**Preparation** You may want to contact an attorney to have him or her explain what some of the different provisions mean or to discuss

some cases in your state that have interpreted the constitutional amendments.

## IMPLEMENTATION

1. Discuss the project with the class. Have students discuss the U.S. Bill of Rights and describe the highlights. Point out the corresponding rights in your state constitution. Encourage students to discuss current events that might involve one of the rights.

2. Organize students into small groups. Distribute copies of the Planning Guidelines, Standards for Evaluating Your Work, and Task Sheet.

3. Review with students the guidelines for doing research.

4. Give students a time frame for finishing the project.

5. Have students work in small groups to divide the state constitution into sections. Identify which sections differ from the U.S. Constitution. Divide the changes or additions among the groups.

6. Determine which group will contact an attorney to come speak to the class. Encourage the students to identify and call the appropriate people.

7. After the students have researched and compared the constitutions, have them collaborate on the pamphlet. Have students organize the pamphlet into categories or by topic. Have them identify the pamphlet's audience. Encourage them to include graphics where they will enhance the material.

8. Have the student groups share what they have learned with the class and input their topic into the pamphlet.

## ASSESSMENT

To evaluate students' work, use the Standards for Evaluating Work on page 15 of this booklet, along with Rubric 42: Writing to Inform and Rubric 9: Comparing and Contrasting in the *Alternative Assessment Handbook* or in a customizable format on the One-Stop Planner.

# Planning Guidelines

In this activity, you will be working in a group with two or three other students to locate the constitution for your state. You will examine your state's constitution to determine if there are any differences between your state rights and those given to citizens of the United States in the Bill of Rights of the U.S. Constitution. Use the library and other resources to research the meaning of the state rights and how they are used. You may get a chance to speak to an attorney about your state constitution. Your goal for this activity is to identify the differences between your rights under the U.S. Constitution and your rights under your state constitution. For example, the Sixth Amendment to the U.S. Constitution guarantees to an accused the right to a speedy trial by an impartial jury. Under Article I, Section 22 of the Florida Constitution, a jury shall consist of not fewer than six people. In comparing the two rights, you could say that there is a right to a jury trial given in both constitutions. However, in Florida, a jury must consist of at least six people. That requirement is not given in the U.S. Constitution.

You should think about what the differences between the U.S. and state constitutions mean and how they affect the lives of citizens in your state. You will create a pamphlet telling newly arrived persons, such as immigrants, college students, or others, what rights they have under your state constitution that may be different from those under the U.S. Constitution. Your pamphlet should include pictures or other graphics to make your pamphlet easier to understand and more interesting.

1. Decide what resources you will use to locate the state constitution.

2. Examine the state constitution and find those rights that are similar to the Bill of Rights found in the U.S. Constitution. Discuss with your group what the rights mean. Try to determine how they affect your rights in a way that may be different from how the U.S. Constitution affects your rights.

3. If you are having an attorney speak to your class, think of questions to ask him or her that you might use in your pamphlet. You might want to ask the attorney what kinds of things people who are new to your state would need to know in order to be good citizens. Prepare the questions ahead of time and listen carefully to the answers. Have a member of your group take notes so that you have the answers written down.

4. Create a pamphlet advising new citizens of your state of their rights under your state constitution. Look at some other pamphlets to see what information they include and how it is organized. Think of some pictures that you might use to illustrate the points you make in the pamphlet.

# Standards for Evaluating Work

## EXCELLENT

- Research includes the state constitution and many sources of information about what the amendments mean. Sources are thoroughly documented. The questions for the speaker are designed to elicit information that helps the student understand how the rights under the state constitution differ from those under the U.S. Constitution.

- The information students gather about the amendments they are assigned to study is accurate and shows an understanding of the amendments and how they affect the lives of citizens.

- The part of the pamphlet students are assigned to create is well written and well organized. It contains information about what the amendment says and how it affects people's lives. It contains graphics that are relevant and illustrative.

## ACCEPTABLE

- Research includes the state constitution and several different sources of information about what the amendments mean. Students' questions for the speaker show some understanding of the issues raised by the amendment.

- The information students gather about the amendments is generally accurate and will be acceptable to include in the pamphlet but will not inform the new citizen of the differences between his or her rights under the state constitution and rights under the U.S. Constitution.

- The information included in the pamphlet is fairly well organized and clear. The pamphlet contains some interesting information, and the graphics are related to the material.

## UNACCEPTABLE

- Research is poor and provides little information. Sources are few. Students' questions for the speaker are not designed to further an understanding of the rights and do not help in understanding the effect on citizens.

- The new information gathered about the amendments is inaccurate and does not inform a new citizen of any of his or her rights under the state constitution.

- The material prepared for the pamphlet is unorganized and not clearly written. There are no graphics or the graphics are unrelated to the material provided.

Name _____ Class _____ Date _____

## Task Sheet

Check off the following tasks as you complete the activity.

❑ **1.** Obtain a copy of the state constitution.

❑ **2.** Research background information that tells you what rights the state's constitution gives you and how those rights are used in the lives of the people in your state.

❑ **3.** Contact an attorney who will speak to your class about your state constitution. Prepare questions to ask about the amendments you are assigned to write about in your pamphlet.

❑ **4.** Create your pamphlet for advising new citizens about their rights under the state constitution. Choose graphics that help to illustrate your points and describe how the citizen could use those rights in everyday life. Compare the rights under the U.S. Constitution with the rights under the state constitution to show that the citizen has different rights or more rights.

# Rate Your Legislator

## OBJECTIVES

After completing this activity, students will be able to:

- Identify the legislators who represent their interests in the House of Representatives.
- Discuss the voting record of their legislators and recognize the importance of accountability.
- Write a letter to their legislators discussing their voting records.

## OVERVIEW

In this activity, students will investigate the voting records of their legislators in the U.S. House of Representatives. Students will obtain a districting map of their state and contact their congressional representatives. Students will also research the voting records of their legislators from the last session of Congress to determine how their legislators voted on key issues selected by the students. The students will then write to their legislators to express their opinions about their voting records.

## PLANNING

**Suggested Time** Plan to spend at least two 45-minute class periods and two homework assignments on this activity.

**Resources** Students should be able to find information about members of the House of Representatives from the Web site of the U.S. Congress or the local telephone directory. A districting map is available from most county voter registration offices, the public library, or your state's Web site. Legislative voting records are available on the Web site of the U.S. Congress, and from legislators' offices or other state agencies.

**Preparation** Your state may be too large for students to research all the representatives. If so, you may divide this assignment by region and research only parts of your state, or focus on the representative from the district in which your school is located.

## IMPLEMENTATION

1. Discuss the project with the class. You might begin by asking students to think about who represents their interests directly in Congress. Then distribute copies of the Planning Guidelines, Standards for Evaluating Work, and Task Sheet to students. Review these materials with the class, giving students a time frame for completing their research and writing their letters to their legislators.

2. When the students understand the assignment, organize them into teams. The number of teams should be the same as the number of legislative districts you will be studying. Assign each team to research one legislator.

3. Have students begin the research by obtaining a map of legislative districts and identifying the members of the U.S. House of Representatives from their state or the regions they are studying. Tell them to obtain voting records by contacting the representatives directly or consulting congressional records.

4. Students should select the issues for comparison. Then they should determine how their legislators voted on these issues, as well as the number of times the legislators did not vote or were absent from voting during the last session of Congress.

5. When each group has finished their research, they should write a letter to their legislators expressing their opinions of the records and explaining whether they feel the legislators are doing a good job.

6. Have teams compare the ratings they gave to the legislators. Then have them explain their evaluations and discuss the ratings.

## ASSESSMENT

To evaluate students' work, use the Standards for Evaluating Work on page 19 of this booklet, along with Rubric 5: Business Letters, and Rubric 12: Drawing Conclusions in the *Alternate Assessment Handbook* or in a customizable format on the One-Stop Planner.

## Planning Guidelines

In this activity, you will be working in small groups to evaluate the legislators elected to represent your state in the House of Representatives. You will learn how these elected officials voted during the most recent term in Congress on certain key issues that you will select. After determining who represents you in the U.S. Congress and the key issues, you can then compare the voting records of your legislators on these issues. Then you can rate the legislators based on how they voted and whether you feel they did a good job representing your interests. After rating your legislator, write a letter to them expressing your opinions of their performance during the past congressional term. Finally, you will compare your legislator's voting record with those of the other legislators assigned to the rest of the class. You may want to share those ratings with the legislators to whom you write.

1. You should first obtain the names of the legislators who represent your state. Determine which legislator you will evaluate.

2. Research the issues addressed in the most recent congressional session that your class identified as important. Find out how your legislator voted on those issues.

3. Along with other students in your class, develop a rating system to use for all the legislators. Rate your legislator using this system.

4. Be sure to include the number of times your legislator did not vote (abstained) or was absent on the day votes were taken.

5. Through this activity, you will learn how important your legislator's vote is in Congress, how to hold your elected officials accountable for their actions, and how to rate the effectiveness of elected officials. You also will learn how to write to your legislators in Washington, D.C., expressing your opinions about their work.

# Standards for Evaluating Work

## EXCELLENT

- Research is complete and the student uses the correct sources for compiling information about the legislators who represent them in the U.S. House of Representatives.

- The votes are correctly and completely tallied and the rating is reasonable. The data supports the student's letter.

- The letter to the legislator is well written. It expresses accurately the record of the legislator and contains well-reasoned opinions about how the student feels about the legislator's record.

## ACCEPTABLE

- Research is adequate in identifying the members of the House of Representatives from your state or region.

- The votes are tallied correctly and the rating system is used properly.

- The letter to the legislator is adequate. The opinions expressed are supported by the data collected.

## UNACCEPTABLE

- Research does not provide information about who represents the student in the House of Representatives. Sources are not used correctly or thoroughly.

- The voting record is inaccurate or incomplete. The rating system is not used properly.

- The letter is poorly written and does not express an opinion about the legislator's voting record.

Name _____ Class _____ Date _____

## Task Sheet

Check off the following tasks as you complete the activity.

❑ **1.** Obtain the names of the legislators who represent your state in the U.S. House of Representatives.

❑ **2.** Research the issues that Congress addressed in its most recent session. Decide which issues you want to use to compare the legislators' voting records.

❑ **3.** Develop a rating system along with your classmates so each legislator is compared using the same system.

❑ **4.** Conduct research on the voting records of your legislator on the issues you've selected. Be sure to include the abstentions and absentee votes.

❑ **5.** Rate your legislator using the rating system developed by the class.

❑ **6.** Write a letter to your legislator expressing and explaining your opinion about their voting record.

## The Executive Branch

# "...Ask What You Can Do..."

## OBJECTIVES

After completing this activity, students will be able to:

• Describe the purpose of the Peace Corps.

• Discuss the value of public service and volunteerism.

• Prepare an application for acceptance into the Peace Corps.

## OVERVIEW

In this activity, students will research the Peace Corps. Founded in 1961 by President John F. Kennedy, Peace Corps volunteers around the world help with long-term development projects and education in developing countries. Students will research the history of the Peace Corps from its creation by executive order to its current status as an independent agency. Students will also invite a former member of the Peace Corps to come speak to their class. Finally, students will complete applications for admission into the Peace Corps.

## PLANNING

**Suggested Time** Plan to spend at least two 45-minute class periods and two homework assignments on this activity.

**Resources** Students should be able to find information about the Peace Corps by locating its nearest office or visiting its Web site.

**Preparation** The local Peace Corps office can provide applications and assist in finding a former or current volunteer to speak to the class. Students should evaluate their own qualifications as a potential volunteer.

## IMPLEMENTATION

1. Discuss the project with the class. You might begin by asking students to consider their qualifications to be Peace Corps volunteers. Ask them what motivated President Kennedy's inaugural speech that introduced the concept of the Peace Corps. Then distribute copies of the Planning Guidelines, Standards for Evaluating Work, and Task Sheet to students. Review these materials with the class, giving students a time frame for completing their research and their applications.

2. Students can work individually or in groups on this assignment. Have them research the origin of the Peace Corps, its function, and the types of volunteer work it sponsors around the world. Groups may research the development of the organization. Each group can focus on a different topic such as one of the following: the Peace Corps' educational efforts; agricultural programs; international rescue efforts; and domestic programs.

3. Ask students to begin the research by contacting the local Peace Corps office and obtaining application forms. Then ask them to find a Peace Corps volunteer to speak to the class.

4. Students should think about what qualifications they can develop now to prepare themselves for this type of service.

5. When groups have finished their research, have each student complete a Peace Corps application. Discuss with the class their individual qualifications.

## ASSESSMENT

To evaluate students' work, use the Standards for Evaluating Work on page 23 of this booklet, along with Rubric 31: Resumes, and Rubric 40: Writing to Describe in the *Alternative Assessment Handbook* or in a customizable format on the One-Stop Planner.

# Planning Guidelines

In this activity, you will learn about one of the world's premier volunteer organizations—the Peace Corps. You will trace the organizational structure from its formation in 1961 to the present. You will also conduct research on this organization to find out what it does around the world and the types of programs it offers. You will discover in what countries the Peace Corps is based and how many volunteers are working on behalf of the organization. You will also invite a guest speaker to your class to discuss his or her experiences as a Peace Corps volunteer and to give you tips about how to become a Peace Corps volunteer yourself. Lastly, you will complete an application for admission to the Peace Corps and think about yourself as a volunteer.

1. You should first obtain the address of the nearest Peace Corps office and ask them to recommend a former volunteer who could speak to your class.

2. You should then research the origins of the Peace Corps and determine how it was created and its purpose. Your research should include the number of people who have volunteered since 1961 and the role of the Peace Corps in developing countries.

3. Investigate the domestic programs of the Peace Corps (programs in the United States). Determine whether any Peace Corps programs are in your area or region and find out what kind of work they are doing.

4. Write a summary about what you think makes a good volunteer based on what you learn in your research. Write about the qualities and skills you currently have or those you would like to develop if you were going to volunteer. Complete an application for consideration by the Peace Corps.

5. Through this activity, you will learn how many Americans have answered the rhetorical question asked by President Kennedy. You will discover that these volunteers have improved the quality of life for thousands of people in this country and around the world. You will also learn that you too can become a Peace Corps volunteer.

# Standards for Evaluating Work

## EXCELLENT

- Research is complete and the student has thoroughly traced the history of the Peace Corps from its inception to today. The student has listed all of the programs and services the Peace Corps offers.

- The student's self-evaluation is thoughtful and accurate. The student has determined the qualifications needed to be a Peace Corps volunteer and asked relevant questions of the guest speaker.

- The application is completed and contains the student's qualifications to be a volunteer.

## ACCEPTABLE

- Research traces the organization's development, and contains descriptions of some of the programs and services offered by the Peace Corps.

- The student's self-evaluation lists some attributes that pertain to volunteering. The student asked some questions of the guest speaker.

- The application is filled out and contains some information about the student that relates to service in the Peace Corps.

## UNACCEPTABLE

- Research is poor and provides little information on the organization's history. The student has not adequately researched the programs provided by the Peace Corps.

- The student's self-evaluation does not adequately assess qualifications related to volunteering. The student does not participate in questioning the guest speaker.

- The student's application is incomplete or not relevant. The student's application shows little understanding of what is required to volunteer for the Peace Corps.

## Task Sheet

Check off the following tasks as you complete the activity.

☐ **1.** Contact the nearest Peace Corps office to request a guest speaker and application forms.

☐ **2.** Research the history of the Peace Corps. Determine who started it, what branch of government it was originally assigned to, and the status of the agency now.

☐ **3.** Research what the organization does. Find out how many volunteers are a part of the organization, where they serve, what they do, and the nature of their work. Also research its purpose and mission.

☐ **4.** Evaluate your personal qualifications that would be valuable to the Peace Corps. Determine how you might become eligible to serve in the Peace Corps.

☐ **5.** Fill out an application for the Peace Corps. List all your traits and accomplishments that you think would qualify you for service.

# Reaching a Verdict

## OBJECTIVES

After completing this activity, students will be able to:

- Describe how the jury system works.
- Discuss what it means to be innocent until proven guilty.
- Prepare a case for a jury trial.

## OVERVIEW

In this activity, students will prepare a case for trial. Students will prosecute a defendant accused of battery, acting as the attorneys, judge, witnesses, defendant, and jury. The case involves a fight between two students while on school property, and the defense is self-defense. You can choose to use your own state battery and self-defense statutes or use the statute provided. Also included is a set of jury instructions to use as the law. You may want to invite an attorney to act as counsel and judge. Students who are to be jurors should have no involvement in the preparation of the case for either side, nor should the facts be shared with them before the "trial."

## PLANNING

**Suggested Time** Plan to spend at least two 45-minute class periods and three homework assignments on this activity. The actual trial of the case should take no more than 90 minutes.

**Resources** Students may contact and invite an attorney from the public defender's or district attorney's office to assist with the trial. The Mock Trial Association of a local law school or the state bar association may have attorneys who would be willing to help. Finally, a local judge may agree to participate or suggest someone else who would.

**Preparation** Students will have to prepare witnesses for trial, familiarize themselves with the case, and organize arguments. You should delegate the responsibilities and assign roles.

## IMPLEMENTATION

1. Discuss the project with the class. You might begin by asking students to consider the meaning of "a jury of peers" and "innocent until proven guilty." Review the case with the class and give students a time frame for preparing their case for trial.

2. When students understand the facts of the case, organize them into prosecution and defense teams. Then choose the witnesses, judge, and the jury. The jury may consist of as many students as necessary to have full participation.

3. In the beginning of the trial, instruct each side to deliver an opening statement describing what they think the evidence will show. Tell students that the prosecutor begins the trial by questioning the victim. The defense attorney then cross-examines the victim. Tell students that the prosecutor examines the second witness and the defense attorney cross-examines that witness. The prosecution then rests its case. The defense then puts on its case by first calling the defense witness and then the defendant. The same procedure is followed for direct examination by the defense attorney and then cross-examination by the prosecutor. At the end of examination, the prosecutor and defense attorney make closing arguments, urging the jury to convict or acquit, respectively.

4. Before the jury deliberates, but after closing arguments, the judge should read the law to the jurors and instruct them to follow only that law.

5. The jury then deliberates and renders a unanimous verdict.

## ASSESSMENT

To evaluate students' work, use the Standards for Evaluating Work, on page 11 of this booklet along with Rubric 16: Judging Information, Rubric 18: Listening, and Rubric 35: Solving Problems, in the *Alternative Assessment Handbook* or in a customizable format on the One-Stop Planner.

# Planning Guidelines

In this activity, you will conduct a trial. If you are on the prosecution team, take the facts given below and develop questions to ask your witnesses to try to prove your case. These are the only facts you know and the only witnesses you have. If you are on the defense team, look at the facts below and develop questions to ask your witness at trial to try to prove that your defendant used self-defense. If you are a juror, you should not know any of the facts before hearing them at trial. If you are the witnesses for either side, then it is your job to learn the facts and try to be convincing witnesses. Like the jurors, the judge should not be familiar with the facts of the case before the trial as well.

1. Facts: On January 5, Pat and Chris were on the school bus. Chris told Pat that Don had threatened to "flatten him" the next time Don saw him because he saw Pat talking to Robin, a girl Don liked, at the basketball game the night before. Pat had been at the game and talked to Robin about a school assignment. Pat knew Don liked Robin, but he also knew that Robin did not like Don because she told him so when Don walked by the two of them as they were talking. Robin told Pat that she thought Don was a loser and strange because he always stared at her yet never spoke. Pat told Robin that he had heard that Don was "trouble" and she should stay away from him. Later that day, as Pat was changing class, he saw a group of guys approaching him. Don was in the middle of the group and started pointing at Pat. Pat, remembering what Chris had told him on the bus, became afraid. As Don came up to him, Pat picked up his metal lunch box and swung it at Don, hitting him in the head and knocking him unconscious. As it turned out, Don was going to ask Pat if he could get Robin's phone number from him so he could call her; he had no intention of attacking Pat. In fact, Chris had not been honest with Pat. Don had never spoken to Chris and never threatened to "flatten" Pat.

2. The witnesses for the prosecution are Don, the victim, and Stan, Don's friend who saw Pat swing the lunch box and hit Don. The witnesses for the defense are Pat, the defendant who is charged with battery, and Chris. Chris is also a friend of Robin who knew that Don liked Robin, but that Robin liked Pat. Pat did not know Robin liked him.

3. The burden of proof is beyond a reasonable doubt. For battery to be proven, the prosecution must prove that there was an intentional, unpermitted or offensive touching of the body of another by any object or person. The defense must show that Pat was justified in using self-defense. Self-defense is using force to protect oneself from unpermitted touching. A person is justified in using self-defense if he reasonably believes he is in imminent danger of bodily harm. A belief can be reasonable even if it is not real, but there has to be an act committed in furtherance of the threat. Imminent implies a present act, not a future one.

4. If Pat was justified in using self-defense, he is not guilty.

# Standards for Evaluating Work

## EXCELLENT

- Students fully participate in the part of the trial to which they are assigned. If they are attorneys, they fully prepare questions, witnesses, and any arguments they intend to make. If they are witnesses, they fully prepare their testimony for trial and answer the questions in accordance with the facts. If they are jurors, they fully participate in the deliberations.

- The case is thoroughly prepared for trial with opening statements fully developed, witnesses coached, and evidence presented in a logical fashion. Jurors are attentive and appear to understand the facts of the case.

- The trial is conducted in an orderly fashion with both sides presenting their theories of the case and eliciting testimony consistent with those theories. Juror questions and deliberative comments indicate an understanding of the facts, law, and burden of proof.

## ACCEPTABLE

- Students participate in the part of the trial to which they are assigned. If they are attorneys, they somewhat prepare witnesses and arguments. If witnesses, they are prepared to testify and can answer the questions. If jurors, they listen attentively.

- The case is prepared and opening statements are delivered. Witnesses can testify and evidence is admitted. Jurors are attentive and know the facts.

- The trial is conducted and both sides present their cases. Witnesses testify but without the benefit of a cogent theory. Juror's questions lack a complete understanding of facts, law, and burden of proof.

## UNACCEPTABLE

- Students are assigned to certain tasks but are ill-prepared for trial. If attorneys, they have not prepared their cases, witnesses, nor arguments. If witnesses, they have not prepared their testimonies. If jurors, they have not paid attention nor do they understand the facts.

- The case is not well-prepared. It does not have a theme nor do the witnesses testify consistently with the facts of the case. Jurors lack any understanding of what happened, the facts of the case, or the law applied.

- The trial cannot be presented because the students have not prepared arguments, statements, or witnesses. Jurors have no understanding of the procedure for establishing burden of proof.

# Task Sheet

Check off the following tasks as you complete the activity.

❑ **1.** If you are the attorney, prepare an opening statement that tells the jury what you think the evidence will show and what you think the witnesses will say. Try to develop a theme for your case. If you are the witness, work with the attorney to develop your testimony, making it consistent with the facts of the case. If you are the juror, familiarize yourself with the burdens of proof that the state must use in a criminal case.

❑ **2.** If you are the attorney, prepare your witnesses to testify and try to anticipate what the witnesses might expect on cross-examination. If you are the witness, try to anticipate what the attorney who is trying to discredit your story might say on cross-examination and prepare responses that help your side.

❑ **3.** If you are the attorney, prepare a cross-examination for the other side's witnesses and victim or defendant. If you are the defense attorney, how will you cross-examine the victim and his witness? If you are the prosecutor, how will you cross-examine the defendant? If you are the witness, what demeanor should you try to convey to the jury? What would likely cause the jury to believe your story or not?

❑ **4.** If you are the attorney, prepare your closing argument. Think about how you can convince the jury that your side of the case is correct. If you are the witness, help the attorneys develop their strong and weak points so they can highlight or diminish them. What holes did they leave in the story? What's the strongest point?

❑ **5.** If you are the jury, what questions would you like answered by the attorneys or witnesses? What is your verdict? What would you advise either side to do the next time to help you? What is your opinion about burden of proof? Discuss all aspects of the trial with your classmates.

# This Building Has a Name?

## OBJECTIVES

After completing this activity, students will be able to:

• Identify people who have had buildings or structures named after them in their community.

• Discuss the contribution that these people made to the community.

• Determine how a person is chosen for the honor of having a building named after them.

• Create a campaign poster that nominates a person to have a public building named after them.

## OVERVIEW

In this activity, students will identify a group of buildings or structures by their names. You can choose local government buildings, public schools, university buildings, libraries, bridges, or any other structure. Have students research who the buildings are named after and the major contributions those individuals made to the community. Identify how many of these people were members of the state judiciary, executive, or legislative branches of government. Have students research any planned construction of new buildings locally, regionally, or statewide. Have students find out how to nominate a person to have a building named after them. Then have students nominate someone and explain why. Finally, students should create a campaign poster encouraging support for naming a building after their nominees.

## PLANNING

**Suggested Time** Plan to spend at least two 45-minute class periods and two homework assignments on this activity.

**Resources** Students can find the names of public buildings from the local library or the Internet by visiting the Web sites of local, county, state, and federal government, universities, hospitals, and similar institutions.

If students choose to research public schools, they can consult the local school board.

**Preparation** If the buildings are local, a visit to the site might be arranged.

## IMPLEMENTATION

1. Have students identify local buildings that have names attached to them. Have them think of why these buildings have names, and how the people were chosen to have the buildings named after them. Distribute copies of the Planning Guidelines, Standards for Evaluating Work, and Task Sheet. Review these materials and give students a time frame for completing the assignment.

2. Once students have selected the group of buildings to research, organize them into teams. Each team has three tasks. First, students need to identify the people for whom the buildings are named. Second, they need to research who these people were and their main contributions to their communities. Third, students should identify who they would chose to name a new building after and explain why.

3. Students' research should lead them to prominent citizens who were most likely members of the groups studied in this chapter. Students should find that their nominees have a wide variety of experiences and contributions.

4. After the student teams have finished their research as a class, have them decide who they would choose to name the next building after. What contribution has that person made to the community that warrants such consideration?

5. Ask each team to create a poster supporting the person the class nominates.

## ASSESSMENT

To evaluate students' work, use the Standards for Evaluating Work on page 31 of this booklet, along with Rubric 1: Acquiring Information, and Rubric 28: Posters, in the *Alternative Assessment Handbook* or in a customizable format on the One-Stop Planner.

# Planning Guidelines

In this activity, you will discover the people in your community who have their names memorialized on buildings in your community, region, or state. Choose a group of buildings. These buildings can be government buildings, university buildings, libraries, public schools, or even bridges, statues, or parks. What attributes do the people share whose names appear here? What do you think is the significance of having your name permanently memorialized in this way? Are there any similarities among the people these buildings are named for? Where would you begin to look for a person to name a building after? Your goals for this activity are (1) to find the most deserving person who has been overlooked for this recognition, and (2) to recognize the characteristics and contributions of significant members of your community.

1. First, decide on the type of buildings or structures you are going to research. These can be local, regional, or state buildings, but they should all be the same types of buildings or structures.

2. After identifying the buildings or structures, identify the individuals whose names appear on the buildings. Research the background of these individuals. List what you think their major contributions were to their communities that made them worthy of this recognition. How many of these people were former state legislators, judges, or government executives?

3. Research more recent history to determine who else in your state might qualify to have their name appear on a building. What do you think that person's main contribution was that makes him or her an appropriate choice?

4. Find out if there is a building being constructed in your community and whose name, if anyone's, will appear on the building. Create a campaign poster for the person who you think should be on the building. Clearly state why you think that person should be so honored.

5. Through this activity, you will learn about the people who were prominent in your community and their contributions. You will also learn about the process of nominating someone to be honored on a building in your community.

# Standards for Evaluating Work

## EXCELLENT

- Research of the names on the buildings or structures is complete and a variety of resources are used. The persons for whom the buildings are named are thoroughly researched and their primary contributions to their communities are correctly identified.

- The student has thoughtfully considered possible nominees for inclusion. The people listed have made significant contributions and meet the criteria for consideration.

- The campaign poster is creative and includes information needed to convince the public that the person is worthy of consideration and should not be overlooked.

## ACCEPTABLE

- Research includes the names of people on the buildings or structures in the group. There is some research into the main contributions of those people, but gaps in information occur or the information does not include relevant data.

- The student has a list of names of people worthy of consideration, but the names are not of the caliber of people who qualify according to the criteria.

- The campaign poster includes information about the person but is not complete.

## UNACCEPTABLE

- Research is poor and provides little information about the people whose names appear on the buildings or structures, nor are the names completely researched.

- The student has created a list of names but the list is inadequate, or the names are of people who do not qualify according to the rules.

- The campaign poster includes little information about the nominee, and does not explain why the person should be chosen to have a building named after them.

Name _____ Class _____ Date _____

# Task Sheet

Check off the following tasks as you complete the activity.

❑ **1.** Identify the group of buildings that you are going to research. Divide the research among students in your group.

❑ **2.** While you research, take careful notes about the qualifications of the people whose names appear on the buildings. Identify those qualifications and explain what their main contributions were to their communities and why you think these people had buildings named after them. How many of these people were former government executives, legislators, or members of the judiciary?

❑ **3.** Find out what the qualifications are to have a name appear on a building in your community. Before developing a list of potential candidates, do research to find people who you think may have been overlooked who qualify for this honor.

❑ **4.** Find out whether there are any buildings planned for future construction that have not been named, or that are under construction or in planning stages.

❑ **5.** Develop a list of potential candidates whom you think should receive the honor of having a building named after them. What qualifications do they have that makes them worth considering?

❑ **6.** Make a campaign poster that describes the qualifications of your candidate and says why the person should have a building named after them.

# Adopt-A-Highway

## OBJECTIVES

After completing this activity, students will be able to:

- Describe the Adopt-A-Highway program, its beginnings, and the local agency that operates the program in the community.
- Survey the school and students to determine the feasibility of participating in the program.
- Apply for permission to provide this volunteer service.

## OVERVIEW

In this activity, students will conduct research about the Adopt-A-Highway program and determine which local agency handles it for the community. The agency responsible for interstate clean up usually is the state Department of Transportation, but most local or county agencies have similar programs that handle local or county roads. The standard commitment is for two years and at least four clean-up activities per year. Most agencies will provide all the necessary materials, safety equipment, and permits. Volunteers usually have to be at least 12 years of age. Agencies also put up the signs along highways that identify the group that has adopted the stretch of roadway. The adopted stretch is usually two miles long. Students will collect all the information needed to decide whether to participate and apply for a permit, if appropriate.

## PLANNING

**Suggested Time** Plan to spend at least two 45-minute class periods and one homework assignment on this activity.
**Resources** Your state Department of Transportation can be contacted for information about the agency that handles local road clean up.
**Preparation** The school administration will need to decide whether to make the two-year commitment.

## IMPLEMENTATION

1. Discuss the project with the class. You might begin by asking students to consider what benefit this project would have for the school, themselves, and their community.

2. Distribute copies of the the Planning Guidelines, Standards for Evaluating Work, and Task Sheet to the students. Give students a time frame for completing the survey and application process.

3. Assign a student to contact the local, county, or state agency responsible for locally administering the Adopt-A-Highway program.

4. Even if the school decides not to participate in Adopt-A-Highway, the class can still complete the survey and application process. Tells students that information should be obtained from the school administration as to whether the students may, if they wish to, participate in the program. If desired, the county engineer (the person usually responsible for the local program) can be invited to the class to explain the program.

5. When students have obtained the application, have them conduct an informal survey of teachers, students, and school administrators to determine the feasibility of the class or school adopting a local stretch of highway close to your school.

6. If the school decides to adopt the highway, invite the county engineer to speak to the class and provide training. Have the class complete the application.

## ASSESSMENT

To evaluate students' work, use the Standards for Evaluating Work on page 35 of this booklet, along with Rubric 14: Group Activity in the *Alternative Assessment Handbook* or in a customizable format on the One-Stop Planner.

# Planning Guidelines

In this activity, you will be working as a class to learn about the national Adopt-A-Highway program. Research this program by finding how, when, and by whom it was started. Determine what needs it serves and who volunteers. Find out who conducts the program in your community. Contact the local program coordinator to see whether your school can participate. Talk to school administrators to get permission to participate and try to get students to support your volunteer efforts if the school administrators allow it. Conduct a survey, giving the students and teachers information about the program and seek their support. Then complete an application for the program. Even if your school does not permit your class to participate, talk to the program's local coordinators to find out about the local organizations involved and the requirements for participating. Your goal for this activity is to learn about the needs of your community and how you can volunteer to help meet those needs in the areas of road safety, beautification, and clean up.

1. First research the origins of the program nationwide. Then contact officials in your state to determine which agency administers an equivalent program locally. Contact that agency and obtain an application.

2. Next, seek permission from your school for your class to participate in your local program.

3. Prepare a survey explaining all the requirements for the program to gather support for your class to participate.

4. Conduct a survey of students and teachers in your school to determine if they would be interested in participating if school officials will allow it. Conduct the survey even if your school prohibits you from participating.

5. Complete the application process. Through this activity, you have learned that organizations and individuals can participate in many local programs to improve their community.

# Standards for Evaluating Work

## EXCELLENT

- Research on the history of the national Adopt-A-Highway program is complete and correct. The local agency is correctly identified and the proper person is located who can provide information about adopting a local highway.

- The student has an excellent understanding of the task. The student provides a source to contact to seek school approval, has a source for securing the application, and has included pertinent information and questions on the survey to solicit the responses needed.

- The survey is conducted in a logical way. Responses are collected that give good information about the feasibility of participating in the local program. The application is completed correctly.

## ACCEPTABLE

- Research is done on the origins of the national Adopt-A-Highway program but is less than complete or accurate. The local agency that can provide the class with information on the local program is identified.

- The student understands the task. The student has identified the relevant school officials to contact and has completed the survey with pertinent information included.

- The survey is conducted, and the student obtains some information about the feasibility of participating in the local program. The application is completed.

## UNACCEPTABLE

- Research is poor and provides little information on the origins of the national Adopt-A-Highway program. The local agency is not identified.

- The student has a poor understanding of the task. He or she has not identified the school official to apply for approval nor the relevant office necessary to contact for information on the local program. The survey is poorly constructed and does not provide the information necessary to solicit adequate responses on the issue.

- The survey is conducted but does not yield relevant information that can be used to determine the feasibility of participating in the program. The application is completed but contains errors or is incomplete.

## Chapter 9, Community Service and Participation Activity, continued

# Task Sheet

Check off the following tasks as you complete the activity.

❑ **1.** Research information about the origins of the national Adopt-A-Highway program. Tell why it was started and who administers it.

❑ **2.** Locate the local office that administers the same type of program for local roads and highways. What agency is responsible for administering it and whom should you contact about your class participating?

❑ **3.** Contact your school administrator to seek permission to participate in the local program if your classmates choose to do so.

❑ **4.** Invite the local county engineer or other program administrator to your class to describe the program and the responsibilities of participating organizations, such as your class. Obtain an application to adopt a highway.

❑ **5.** Design a survey to give to classmates and teachers in your school to see if they would be interested in participating. Be sure to include all the requirements for adopting a highway so that they can be informed of the responsibilities involved.

❑ **6.** Record the results of the survey. Determine whether you received a positive or negative response to your idea of adopting a highway. If the response is favorable, and the administration allows your class to participate, complete the application. Make sure the application is complete and free from errors. If the survey returns negative results, discuss why that happened with your class. If the administration will not allow your class to participate, discuss that issue with your class.

# Choose Your Party

## OBJECTIVES

After completing this activity, students will be able to:

- Identify the major political parties in their community.
- Describe the party platform for each party.
- Learn how to register to vote.

## OVERVIEW

In this activity, students will visit the local Democratic and Republican Party headquarters and one third-party political office. They will learn the differences among these parties' platforms and the different positions each takes on major issues in the community. Students will examine different campaign materials and learn how a candidate gets elected. Students will also learn the size of their precinct, how parties and candidates urge their constituents to vote, how funds are collected to support the parties' activities, how volunteers help during a campaign, and what exactly occurs when a candidate wins an election. Any political office can be studied. Students may use this information to discuss their own political leanings. Students will obtain voter registration forms to complete.

## PLANNING

**Suggested Time** Plan to spend at least one 45-minute class period and one homework assignment on this activity. Students will also spend time visiting local political offices.

**Resources** Students can obtain voter registration forms from local or state election offices.

**Preparation** You may have to contact party headquarters in writing if no campaigns are currently under way. Some offices are not staffed between elections. However, all parties will make available a staff member to discuss the party. If no staff member is available to visit, invite the local political representative from that party to address the class.

## IMPLEMENTATION

1. Discuss the project with the class. You might begin by asking students to discuss what they know about the parties and how elections are conducted. You also might discuss with students what they know about different issues and what is each party's stand on an issue. Distribute copies of the Planning Guidelines, Standards for Evaluating Your Work, and Task Sheet to the class. Explain to students that they will be visiting the headquarters of the major political parties in their area.

2. Have the class formulate areas of interest about a campaign. Have them write questions to ask the staffs of the offices they visit or the guest speakers they invite to class. Students might be organized into two or three groups to take the lead on addressing the different parties' platforms. Students might also be organized into small groups to handle certain areas, such as campaign finances, volunteerism, campaign materials, and election-day activities.

3. Have students examine the voter registration form. Discuss with them the reasons for each question. Ask them to explain why the voter registration form does not require more extensive information.

4. When the class has completed the office visits (or guest speakers have visited the class), discuss with the class their views on the different parties' platforms. Which party is predominantly represented in your community? What are the political leanings of the members of the class?

## ASSESSMENT

To evaluate students' work, use the Standards for Evaluating Work on page 39 of this booklet, along with Rubric 9: Comparing and Contrasting, and Rubric 12: Drawing Conclusions, in the *Alternative Assessment Handbook* or in a customizable format on the One-Stop Planner.

# Planning Guidelines

In this activity, you will be visiting the local offices of the major political parties in your community. After identifying the two major parties, the Democrats and the Republicans, you will also research other political parties that might exist in your community. When you visit a political party's office, you should be able to see what occurs there. If you visit during an election campaign, you will see how an office runs, what the people who work there do, what information is gathered, what materials are created or used in the campaign, and how the voters are solicited or encouraged to vote. In addition you will be able to see how volunteers are used to help the parties operate. You can also ask about the party's political platform, that is, their position on important public issues. You should ask questions about current or future candidates and see how many of their ideas you agree or disagree with. At the end of your visits, you will register to vote and participate in a class discussion about what political leanings the students have. You will learn which party is the most popular in your community.

1. Before meeting with your small group, determine the most popular party in your community. Also identify a third political party that is lesser known than the two main parties.

2. In your group, discuss how to handle your visit, what kinds of questions to ask, what issues to learn about, and who in your group will be responsible for collecting and asking the questions. You might divide the task into components, with one person asking about financing, one about volunteers, etc. Make a list of all the questions you want answered.

3. When you visit the offices, look around. Note what you see. What kind of office is it? Are there many people around? What are they doing? Is there a campaign currently underway? What literature do you see?

4. Ask questions of the person addressing your group. What is the party's position on the issues you have identified? You might ask what statistics are gathered by the party's office. How much information do they have about the voters?

5. After you complete your visit, discuss with the class your opinions about what you learned. What are some differences between parties? Are the differences significant? What is your political leaning?

6. After obtaining a voter registration form, fill it out. What questions does it ask? Why does the agency registering you to vote need to know the information asked for on the form?

# Standards for Evaluating Work

## EXCELLENT

- Student is aware of and has participated in selecting the main and third-party political offices to visit. The questions developed for the visits to the political offices are relevant and show an interest and complete understanding of political parties and the voting and campaigning process.

- The student's participation at the political offices is excellent. The student observes all aspects of the office and asks cogent questions that help to illuminate the inner workings of the office. The student has excellent questions about the issues chosen to be addressed and asks good follow-up questions.

- The student completely and correctly fills out the voter registration card. The student participates in the discussion about why the card asks for certain information and why it is necessary to register to vote. The student has identified his or her political leanings based on an understanding of the parties' platforms on issues. The student's position is well-reasoned.

## ACCEPTABLE

- Student has been somewhat helpful in identifying the political parties in the community. The student's questions are cogent and cover some aspects of the task. Student shows an interest in the political system and a grasp of the voting and campaign process.

- Student has good participation at the political offices. Student observes and understands most of what the office reveals. Student has good questions about the issues and understands the purpose and workings of the political headquarters.

- Student fills out the voter registration form correctly. Student participates in the discussion about why the card asks for certain information but does not show a complete understanding of the issues. Student has identified his or her political leanings but cannot fully support them.

## UNACCEPTABLE

- Student's input into identifying the political parties is minimal and the student is unable to contribute to choosing the third-party office to visit. The questions add little to understanding the political process and what voting and campaigning involves.

- Student participates little or not at all while visiting the office. Student does not ask questions about the issues and does not understand the workings of the office.

- Student fills out the voter registration card, but it is not complete or correct. Student barely participates in the discussion about the importance of the card. Student cannot identify his or her political leanings, and cannot support these leanings with reasons.

Name _____ Class _____ Date _____

## Task Sheet

Check off the following tasks as you complete the activity.

❏ **1.** Obtain the addresses of the political parties in your community for the Democratic, Republican, and one other party. Choose a time to visit these headquarters.

❏ **2.** In your small group, develop questions to be answered by the staffs at the offices you visit. Divide the task of developing the questions into categories, such as campaign finances, volunteerism, getting out the vote, etc. Develop questions to ask about the party's position on certain key issues that you identify.

❏ **3.** Visit the offices and collect as much data as you can while there. Make notes about what you learn and about the political party's position on issues that you have identified.

❏ **4.** Obtain a voter registration card and fill it out. Discuss with your classmates the questions on that card and the reason the information is needed.

❏ **5.** Have a class discussion on the political parties and what you learned. What were the differences in their positions on the issues you identified? What tactics did they use to contact voters and get their candidates known? Based on what you learned, what kind of voting patterns does your community generally exhibit? Are you persuaded to join one party over the other? Why? What have you learned about your community's voters? Would you help on a political campaign? Why or why not?

# Do Not Believe the Hype

## OBJECTIVES

After completing this activity, students will be able to:

- Identify types of propaganda.
- Discuss propaganda in their community that is directed toward them.
- Determine the effectiveness of propaganda.

## OVERVIEW

In this activity, students will identify propaganda in their community. For three to five days, each time they see a piece of propaganda, they are to write down and record certain facts and impressions about it in a log created for that purpose. At the end of the designated period, students will categorize the propaganda into one of the six types listed in the chapter. Students will then collectively attempt to discern the message the propaganda is intended to convey and rate its effectiveness. Students will choose one piece that they designate as especially effective and write a letter to the source of the message and a letter to the editor of the local newspaper explaining how the piece affected them.

## PLANNING

**Suggested Time** Plan to spend at least two 45-minute class periods and two homework assignments on this activity. Students will carry a log with them for three to five days in preparation for this activity.

**Resources** Students can use any source available, including newspapers, magazines, billboards, television, books, or radio.

**Preparation** You may want to have students look at examples of propaganda to help them identify it. You may choose current examples or use historical examples, such as the government propaganda to end prohibition.

## IMPLEMENTATION

1. Discuss the project with the class. You might begin by asking students to think of an example for each type of propaganda listed in the chapter. Their examples do not have to be confined to political issues but can encompass other types of advertisements with which they might be more familiar. Distribute copies of the Planning Guidelines, Standards for Evaluating Your Work, and Task Sheet to the class. Give the students a time frame for completing the project.

2. Have students create a log in which to record their findings for a time period of three to five days. The log should include a place to describe the propaganda; the facts included in it, if any; the impression the student received from the piece; and the effectiveness of the message. Organize students into groups of three or four and have them record their findings in the log for the designated period of time.

3. When the groups reconvene, have them divide their findings among the categories of propaganda and rate the pieces from most to least effective.

4. After groups have finished this task, have them present their examples to the other students. As a class, decide which example is the most effective. Then have students write a letter to the source of the propaganda and to the editor of the local newspaper expressing their opinions about its effectiveness and explaining their feelings about it.

## ASSESSMENT

To evaluate students' work, use the Standards for Evaluating Work on page 43 of this booklet, along with Rubric 15: Journals, Rubric 17: Letters to Editors, and Rubric 41: Writing to Express, in the *Alternative Assessment Handbook* or in a customizable format on the One-Stop Planner.

# Planning Guidelines

In this activity, you will be working in small groups to learn about the propaganda that influences how the people in your community think and feel about things or people. You will gather information from sources you observe in your community that may be positive or negative and that meet the definition of propaganda as defined in the chapter. You will keep a log of the sources you see and compare with the other students the propaganda that you identify. After evaluating these sources, your class will choose the best example and express an opinion to your community via letters to the editor of a local newspaper and to the source of the propaganda. You will learn what influences different populations in your community and what methods are used for different effects.

1. Before meeting with your small group, develop a log. This log should have a place for you to document each instance of propaganda that you encounter over the period of time that you are assigned to collect this data. In the log should be a space for you to document the place where you saw the item, a description of it, whatever facts, opinions, etc., were expressed in it, and your feelings about it as you saw it. You can include anything else you think might be important. The log can be as simple as you want to make it, and may just be a small notebook. The important thing is that everyone collects the same types of information.

2. In your small group, discuss what kinds of propaganda you will be looking for and try to think of sources that might contain that type of propaganda. For example, newspapers, magazines, billboards, and flyers might be good sources, but other sources may be available, especially if an election is under way in your community.

3. Keep your log with you at all times and record every piece of propaganda that you see fits your categories. Be sure to record how you feel about what you see and whether it has a negative or positive impact, or whether it has no emotional effect. You should record your findings for about three to five days.

4. Meet with your group and compare your logs. Compare your entries and see how many different items you have. If more than one of you recorded the same items, compare the emotional responses you described. Discuss any differences. Categorize the propaganda items into the groupings listed in your chapter. Rate the effectiveness of the items, and choose the most effective.

5. Present your group's selections to the class. After each group has presented its selections, as a class vote on the most and least effective. Decide, as a class, which item you want to write about. Then write a letter to the editor of your local newspaper, telling him or her why you chose the item, what you thought about it, and what made it effective. Write a similar letter to the source of the propaganda.

# Standards for Evaluating Work

## EXCELLENT

- Student has participated fully in creating the log and understands the task. The log has entries that help to document the propaganda. The log is brought back with complete results that add to the overall task.

- Student has valuable insights into the messages conveyed in the propaganda and can articulate those messages. Student also can identify the type of propaganda used in the message. Student has used a variety of sources in collecting data.

- Student contributes important data to the letters to the editor and source, identifying in precise terms the type of propaganda, the category it belongs to, and exactly why it is the best example.

## ACCEPTABLE

- Student has helped to create the log. Student has some entries in the log, but entries are off-subject or incomplete. Logs have some value, but are not very helpful in adding to the overall task.

- Student has some insight into the messages but is unable to articulate the motivation behind the messages or identify the type for each item. Student has not collected items from a variety of sources but has relied on just a few.

- Student contributes somewhat to the letters to the editor and source but lacks insight into what makes the chosen item effective. The student does not have a good grasp of the level of influence contained in the item.

## UNACCEPTABLE

- Student's input into creating the log indicates a lack of understanding of the overall task. Student's log does not have sufficient entries or is incomplete.

- Student has little or no appreciation of the type of propaganda he or she has collected. The student cannot identify the category of propaganda and has not used many sources.

- Student contributes little to the letters to the editor and source. Student has not correctly categorized the item selected and does not have a grasp of the influence of the item and its intended audience or purpose.

# Task Sheet

Check off the following tasks as you complete the activity.

❑ **1.** Create a log to be used by each group member to document each item of propaganda seen during the observation period.

❑ **2.** Meet with your small group to discuss the types of propaganda you are looking for.

❑ **3.** Observe your community for three to five days for different types of propaganda displayed on or in as many different sources as you can find. Record each item you find, filling out the log completely.

❑ **4.** Meet in your small group and compare the items from each student's log. Make a list of all of the different sources and then rate them from most effective to least effective. Discuss with your group why you have rated the items this way, and decide which item your group will present to the class.

❑ **5.** As a class, decide which item of propaganda is either the most effective or least effective. Compose a letter to the editor of your newspaper and the source of the propaganda. Explain what effect the item had on your class, why you think it was very effective, and whether that piece of propaganda should be continued or eliminated. Be sure to defend your position in your letter. Give the editor all of the information that he or she needs about the piece, including what type of propaganda it is, what effect it had on the majority of the students who viewed it, what your emotional response was to the item, whether it contained facts or opinion, and whether the class thought it met the goal intended by the creator of the item. Pay attention to grammar, spelling, and punctuation.

# Pay Your Taxes!

## OBJECTIVES

After completing this activity, students will be able to:

• Describe the difference between federal and state taxes.

• Identify and complete an IRS 1040 short form and a state tax form.

• Discuss what happens to their tax dollars.

## OVERVIEW

In this activity, students will pay their taxes using an IRS 1040 form. Students will begin by obtaining the necessary forms. Forms can easily be downloaded from the Internet. Assign students a salary and standard deductions from a typical workplace, such as McDonalds. Assign each student a slightly different amount of income and deductions. Have them complete the tax forms using the tax tables. Students should research how much of their tax dollar goes to two services that are supported by taxes. One of the services should be supported by state taxes, and the other by federal taxes. For example, how much of the federal tax dollar goes to support the criminal justice system or education? How much of the state tax dollar goes to support those same things locally? Students should research how a taxpayer can object to his or her taxes paying for services or programs he or she does not wish to support.

## PLANNING

**Suggested Time** Plan to spend at least one 45-minute class period and two homework assignments on this activity.

**Resources** Students can obtain a current IRS 1040 form and state tax forms from any local source such as the public library, or they can be downloaded from the Internet.

**Preparation** You may want to use a typical student salary for your area along with deductions as an example. Any dollar figure can be used to calculate the amount of taxes to be paid.

## IMPLEMENTATION

1. Discuss this project with the class. You might begin by asking students whether they think they should pay taxes. If they give a resounding "no," then ask them who should. Get them to identify public services that benefit them (e.g., public parks and recreation) and ask who should pay for them. Distribute copies of the Planning Guidelines, Standards for Evaluating Your Work, and Task Sheet to the class. Give the students a time frame for completing the project.

2. Have students obtain the necessary tax forms. (Generic forms are included in the forms section at the back of this book.) Have them research the amount of money collected by the state and federal government in taxes.

3. Have students choose an area of interest to see how much tax money is spent on that program. Students might choose education, defense, or other public programs. Choose both a state program and federal program. Research how much of their tax dollar goes to those programs of interest.

4. Assign each student his or her "salary" and deductions. Have them complete both the state and federal tax forms. For variety, have some students overpay and some underpay their taxes through manipulation of their deductions.

5. Discuss what taxpayers can do if they are unhappy about which programs are being funded by their taxes.

## ASSESSMENT

To evaluate students' work, use the Standards for Evaluating Work on page 47 of this booklet, along with Rubric 1: Acquiring Information and Rubric 11: Discussions, in the *Alternative Assessment Handbook* or in a customizable format on the One-Stop Planner.

# Planning Guidelines

In this activity, you will learn how the federal and state governments allocate your taxes. You will conduct research to find the amount of tax dollars that are allocated to a program you are interested in, such as defense, education, the arts, welfare, or any other program funded by taxes. Two examples should be chosen—one a program funded by state taxes, and the other, a program funded by federal taxes. You also will get to pay your share of taxes by completing federal and state tax forms. After acquiring these forms, your teacher will assign you a salary and deductions, and you can see exactly how the taxpayer completes and files his or her tax return every year. You can then discuss with your classmates what you can do as a taxpayer if you are unhappy with the way the government spends your tax dollars.

1. Begin by researching the federal and state tax allocations. You are looking for information on how the taxes collected by state and local governments get dispersed to certain programs.

2. Obtain a state tax form and IRS 1040 short form from your local IRS office, or any other agency that has forms available for the public to use. You also may download these forms from the Internet.

3. Your teacher will assign you a salary and give you deductions to use in completing your tax forms. Complete your forms and determine whether you are owed money or whether you must pay additional taxes.

4. Choose a program from both the state and federal governments that is funded by taxpayer dollars. Conduct research to find out how much of the taxpayer dollar goes to fund that program.

5. Conduct research to discover what a taxpayer can do if he or she is unhappy with the way either the state or federal governments allocate taxes. How can you influence how your tax dollars are spent?

# Standards for Evaluating Work

## EXCELLENT

- Student has thoroughly researched the federal and state tax allocations and has determined exactly what percentage of the tax dollar gets allocated for specific programs.

- Student has identified two specific programs of interest funded by federal and state taxes, respectively. Student has researched to see what percentage of the total amount of taxes paid gets allocated to those programs.

- The IRS and state tax forms are completed and the taxes are properly calculated. Student has researched what recourse a taxpayer has to protest the way taxes are allocated by the federal or state government. Student fully participates in the discussion concerning taxpayers' protests.

## ACCEPTABLE

- Student has researched the federal and state tax allocations and has some idea of what percentage of the taxes collected goes toward certain programs.

- Student has identified two programs in the federal and state government that get public funding. Student's research into what percentage of tax dollars gets allocated to the program is incomplete or inaccurate.

- The IRS and state tax forms are completed and taxes are calculated, but either the student has miscalculated or the form is incomplete. Student adds somewhat to the discussion about taxpayers' protest rights.

## UNACCEPTABLE

- Student has not completed research into the federal and state allocations of taxes. Student has no idea what percentage of taxes goes toward any program.

- Student has trouble identifying a federal or state program that is funded by taxpayer dollars. Student has not completed research into what percentage of taxpayers' dollars goes into those programs of interest, or has not identified these programs.

- Student does not complete the IRS or state tax form. Student's calculations are incorrect or incomplete, or not done at all. Student does not participate in the discussion concerning taxpayers' rights to protest.

Name _____ Class _____ Date _____

## Task Sheet

Check off the following tasks as you complete the activity.

❑ **1.** Obtain the IRS 1040 short form from your local tax office or from the Internet. Obtain a form for filing state taxes if your state imposes state taxes.

❑ **2.** Do research to find out how the government allocates the taxes collected to the public programs it funds. For example, what percentage goes to fund the military, education, public libraries, etc.?

❑ **3.** Select two programs you are interested in that are funded by taxes. Choose one from the state government and one from the federal government. This can be any program at all. You can choose one that you like or one that you do not like.

❑ **4.** Research how much of the taxpayers' dollars goes to fund those programs. What percentage of the money collected in taxes goes to pay for that program?

❑ **5.** Complete the IRS short form and the state tax form that you obtained, using the salary and deduction figures your teacher gave you.

❑ **6.** Discuss with the class how you could protest the allocation of your tax dollars to a program that you did not support. In what way could you influence the spending of federal and state taxes?

## Citizenship and the Family

# Drowning in Debt

## OBJECTIVES

After completing this activity, students will be able to:

• Discuss the importance of financial security.

• Describe the relationship between income, a budget, and debt.

• Create a budget for their families.

## OVERVIEW

In this activity, students will learn how to maintain a family on a budget. They will find out how to handle income, how to prepare a budget, and how to manage the financial responsibility of supporting a family. Students will contact a representative of the credit bureau and the local consumer credit counseling center to solicit advice about spending and saving money and managing their debt. Students will also obtain applications from two major credit-card companies and determine the interest rates for using the cards. Finally, students will prepare a budget for their families using a standard budget guide available from the Internet or any financial service organization. Students will create a poster with a pie chart showing their incomes and budgets.

## PLANNING

**Suggested Time** Plan to spend at least two 45-minute class periods and two homework assignments on this activity.

**Resources** Students can find a recommended budget guide on the Internet, from a lending institution, or from most office supply stores. An application for a credit card can be obtained by calling the toll-free number for the card company or from a bank. The local consumer credit counseling center and credit bureau can be contacted via telephone.

**Preparation** You may want to obtain the forms before beginning this segment as well as the names of the nearest credit bureau or consumer counseling center for the students to use.

## IMPLEMENTATION

1. Discuss the project with the class. You might begin by asking students to tell you what they would spend their money on if they could. You might have them discuss what they know about saving money and living on a budget. Distribute copies of the Planning Guidelines, Standards for Evaluating Your Work, and Task Sheet to the class. Give the students a time frame for completing the project.

2. Have students research what normally is included in a family budget and divide their resources accordingly. Have students work in pairs to develop a budget for their family. Make some pairs single-income and others two-income families. Include such expenses as alimony or child support payments, student loans, car payments, insurance costs, and cell phone bills. You can also create exigent circumstances, such as one spouse having been laid off recently or the unexpected costs associated with having to care for aging parents.

3. Invite the speakers to discuss the importance of establishing good credit and managing money. Also ask them to discuss savings and investments and how to avoid excessive debt.

4. Have students examine the credit-card applications. How do you calculate interest? Have students discuss the dangers of creating debt using credit cards. Have them figure out how long it would take to pay off a card charged to the maximum. Have students create a budget using a pie chart.

## ASSESSMENT

To evaluate students' work, use the Standards for Evaluating Work on page 51 of this booklet, along with Rubric 7: Charts and Rubric 28: Posters in the *Alternative Assessment Handbook* or in a customizable format on the One-Stop Planner.

# Planning Guidelines

In this activity, you will be working in pairs to plan a family budget. You will begin by researching what expenses are typical for a family and what percentage of your salary should be allocated for those expenses. You will talk to a representative from the credit bureau to learn what kind of information is contained on your credit report, what it's used for, and how to maintain a favorable rating. You will also talk to a representative of a local consumer credit counseling center for information about how to avoid financial trouble. You will obtain credit-card applications and calculate their interest rates and how much an item actually costs if purchased on credit and then paid off over a longer period of time than the month or so between credit-card statements. You will record your budget using a pie chart.

1. Start by researching what goes into personal budgeting. Find out what the usual costs of maintaining a household are and how much of your money should be placed into savings regularly.

2. Obtain your "salary" and list of special expenses from your teacher.

3. Contact a consumer credit counselor from a local agency that provides debt counseling and a representative from the nearest credit bureau. Make an appointment with their offices or invite them to come speak to the class. Prepare questions concerning credit in general, maintaining a credit history, and how to manage debt.

4. With the information that you obtain from your visit or guest speakers, plan a budget with your partner that takes into consideration all the expenses of your household. How much debt are you in? How will you pay off your debt? What are your plans for investing? Can you send your children to college? Do you have money set aside for an emergency?

5. When you have finished with your budget, prepare a poster depicting your budget. Illustrate your budget as a pie chart showing what percentages of your income is allocated to each expense. What is your prognosis for the future? Can you afford to have children or more children? Are you prepared for retirement? For emergencies? For disaster? Does your spouse need to work? Can you afford to be laid off? Look at the other pairs' budgets. Is your budget realistic?

# Standards for Evaluating Work

## EXCELLENT

- Research includes all information needed to understand how to create a budget and manage a family household. Budget is complete and includes all necessary components.

- Student's questions are thorough and relevant. Questions are designed to elicit information concerning how to address credit and what is needed to maintain a good credit rating. Student takes copious notes and has an excellent understanding of financial management and planning.

- The prepared budget is an excellent financial management tool. All components of budgetary planning are contained and accounted for in the chart. The chart displays a plan that is workable and financially successful.

## ACCEPTABLE

- Research includes information on creating a budget. Research goes into some detail about what is necessary to manage a household.

- Student's questions address the issues of credit and debt management. Student's notes are good. There is some understanding of financial planning and management.

- The prepared budget is good. The components are contained in the pie chart and the budget is workable. The budget can support the household.

## UNACCEPTABLE

- Research includes some information on how to create a budget but is incomplete. Budget components are missing or budget is unrealistic.

- Student's questions are poor. Questions show little understanding of the issues of credit and money management. Student's notes are poor, and there is little information that can be utilized to prepare a family budget.

- The budget is unrealistic and omits necessary components. The pie chart is incomplete and the budget is incapable of maintaining a household.

## Task Sheet

Check off the following tasks as you complete the activity.

- ❑ **1.** Obtain the budget and description of your family and household expenses from your teacher.

- ❑ **2.** Research what it takes to run a household. Pay particular attention to the necessary and customary household expenses, such as rent or mortgage, utilities, and insurance.

- ❑ **3.** Contact the representatives from your local credit bureau and consumer credit counseling agency. Make an appointment to visit their offices or invite them to speak to your class.

- ❑ **4.** Develop questions to ask these individuals that will help you understand how credit functions and how to stay out of debt. Ask what you need to know to come up with a successful budget for your household.

- ❑ **5.** Along with your partner, examine your household. With the income you have been assigned and the specific circumstances of your family, devise a budget that will support you and your household. Identify your specific needs and how you will address them. Try to account for all your budgetary needs, including savings and interest on credit cards.

- ❑ **6.** Illustrate your budget using a pie chart. Draw your pie chart on a poster. Discuss with other members of your class how they addressed certain issues. Observe how they created their budgets and how they planned for the future.

# Each One, Reach One, Teach One

## OBJECTIVES

After completing this activity, students will be able to:

- Identify a preschool, elementary school, or social service agency in their community that accepts donations of children's books.
- Collect books to give to the organization.
- Organize a reading day for the organization.

## OVERVIEW

In this activity, students will identify an organization in their community that is in need of or will accept a donation of books from the class. Students will organize a book donation drive in your school. Each student in the school will be asked to donate their favorite children's book to the drive. Students will organize volunteer parents or others to deliver the books to the school. On that day, the students will go to the organization and put on a play based on a book they have selected. The students will dress up and act as the characters in the book. Students can then interact with the children, reading a book or two to each child individually or in small groups.

## PLANNING

**Suggested Time** Plan to spend at least one 45-minute class period and one homework assignment on this activity. Students will also make a visit to a school or organization.

**Resources** Students can ask the administration for help in collecting the books by having book donation centers located throughout the school. Students can bring a book from home to donate, purchase the books, or solicit from family and friends.

**Preparation** You may want to prepare a list of organizations for the students to choose from if the need is great in your community.

## IMPLEMENTATION

1. Discuss the project with the class. Ask students to think of a book to act out and how to make the characters interesting and fun. Have students think about the age group they will have as an audience and select a book that is age-appropriate. Distribute copies of the Planning Guidelines, Standards for Evaluating Your Work, and Task Sheet to the class. Give students a date for the drive and the visit.

2. Have students create a flyer or advertisement which solicits books from classmates, teachers, and staff at the school. Identify the organization or school to which the books will be donated. Make sure the drop-off points are clearly marked and identified. Organize a pick-up team and a central storage location.

3. Choose the book to be acted out and the students who will be in the cast. Have the other students be the audience, help make costumes, write the dialogue, practice, and critique the performances.

4. Contact the organization to pick a date and time for the presentation. Organize the trip so the maximum number of children can participate and benefit from the contact.

5. Present the play to the children at the preschool, elementary school, or organization. Distribute the other books and talk to the children about the benefits of reading, staying in school, and helping others.

## ASSESSMENT

To evaluate students' work, use the Standards for Evaluating Work on page 55 of this booklet, along with Rubric 14: Group Activity and Rubric 33: Skits and Reader's Theater in the *Alternative Assessment Handbook* or in a customizable format on the One-Stop Planner.

# Planning Guidelines

In this activity, you will be working in one of several groups to collect children's books for a preschool, elementary school, or child-care organization in your community. As part of the gift, your class will also entertain the children by putting on a play adapted from one of the books. Also, on the day you visit the school or organization, you will read one of the donated books to a child or group of children. You will also spend time discussing with them the value and benefit of learning to read, staying in school, and studying hard. Group tasks will include collecting the books donated from other students, teachers, and staff of the school; soliciting volunteers to deliver the books; selecting the book and acting in the play; and preparing costumes and providing other support services. All students will participate in reading individually to the children while visiting the school or organization.

1. Identify the preschool or child-care organization that will accept a donation of books. Emphasis should be placed on an organization that is in need, that focuses on at-risk children, or whose budget is not sufficient to support the purchase of books for its children.

2. Contact the organization and coordinate the activity. Select a time and date for the event. Then select a group of students to organize the collection of the books. Display posters or solicit students, teachers, and staff to donate one book of their choice to the project. Drop-off or collection points should be clearly marked. Collections should be made in a timely manner and the books should be stored securely.

3. The students who are going to perform should select the book from which to adapt a play. Other students should help with creating dialogue, creating costumes, and providing props. The play should be creative and fun for small children.

4. On the day of the visit to the school or child care organization, volunteers will be needed to deliver the books. A group of students should organize the volunteers so the books can be delivered to the school at a convenient time.

5. Present the play. After it's over, each student should choose a child and a book, and read the book to the child individually, talking to him or her about the importance of learning to read, staying in school, and studying. After the trip, discuss with your class how you felt about participating and whether you would do something like this again.

# Standards for Evaluating Work

## EXCELLENT

- Student has participated in locating an appropriate school or organization that has a need for books.

- Student was extremely active in whatever group he or she was assigned. If charged with collecting books, student solicited from many sources and was dedicated to the task. If assigned to seek volunteers for delivery, he or she was successful in getting volunteers from many sources. If part of the play, student took his or her role seriously and practiced diligently.

- Student was animated when reading to a child. Student interacted with his or her assigned child and gave thoughtful, age-appropriate advice.

## ACCEPTABLE

- Student has helped in identifying the school or organization in need of books.

- Student was somewhat active in the group to which he or she was assigned. Student took his or her task seriously but did no more than the minimum to carry out his task.

- Student read to the assigned child, but was not animated nor very interested. Interaction was limited.

## UNACCEPTABLE

- Student was not helpful in identifying an appropriate school or organization for the donation.

- Student was reluctant to volunteer for any of the assigned tasks. When the student was assigned to a group, he or she did not perform well and the task was left to others in the group.

- Student read to the assigned child, but did so without any enthusiasm or interest. No advice was given to the child, nor was there much interaction between the two.

Name _____ Class _____ Date _____

# Task Sheet

Check off the following tasks as you complete the activity.

❑ **1.** Obtain the names of schools or child-care organizations in your community in need of and willing to accept books from your class. Of those that you gather, decide which one needs your help the most.

❑ **2.** After you select the school, your teacher will divide up the tasks that need to be performed. Perform the task you are assigned. If you are in the book collection group, make posters, flyers, or announcements for your school that identify the organization you are going to help and ask for donations of books. If you are in the group assigned to collect the books, get the school administration to identify appropriate drop-off points for collecting the books. Make sure you collect the books and safely store them. If you are chosen to act in the play, select the story and practice your part diligently. If you are in the play support group, prepare costumes and props needed to put on the play. If your group is assigned to organize volunteers to deliver the books, get as many volunteers as needed to complete the task.

❑ **3.** On the day of the trip, be as supportive as you can be to the cast members and make sure the play goes well. Interact with the children in the school and choose a book that you think a child will enjoy. Make sure the book is age appropriate and will appeal to the child.

❑ **4.** After the play is completed, select a child and read your book to him or her. Talk to the child about the value of learning to read, staying in school, and studying hard.

❑ **5.** Have a class discussion on the importance of participating in the community and especially with those less fortunate. Discuss how the visit went and how you think the children enjoyed meeting your class. Think of other ways that your school can make a contribution in your community.

## Citizenship in the Community

# Host a Special Olympian

## OBJECTIVES

After completing this activity, students will be able to:

• Identify athletes in their community who participate in the Special Olympics.

• Research the origins of the Special Olympics and the people it serves.

• Discuss the benefits of participating in the Special Olympics in their community.

## OVERVIEW

In this activity, students will research the Special Olympics. They will discover its origins, who founded the organization, and the purpose it serves. Research should include the local branch or organization that sponsors the Special Olympics in your community. The local organization can provide a speaker and a Special Olympian to visit the class to discuss the events and how the organization supports disabled athletes. Students can examine the stereotypes associated with the disabled and discover whether they share those beliefs. Students can also learn how they can participate and help with the Special Olympics in their area. Students will create a display for the school that highlights the accomplishments of Special Olympians and the Special Olympics.

## PLANNING

**Suggested Time** Plan to spend at least two 45-minute class periods and two homework assignments on this activity. One class will be for the guest speakers.

**Resources** Students can research the Special Olympics using library resources, the local Special Olympics organization, or the Internet.

**Preparation** You may want to call the local chapter of the Special Olympics to determine whether an athlete can visit your class. If an athlete is not available in your area, you may be able to locate a video that discusses the Special Olympics.

## IMPLEMENTATION

1. Discuss the idea of volunteering with the class. Get them to talk about the volunteer organizations they are familiar with and the services they provide. Talk about the role of athletes in society and the concept of having a healthy body. Distribute copies of the Planning Guidelines, Standards for Evaluating Your Work, and Task Sheet to the class. Give the students a time frame for completing the project.

2. Have students research the origins of the Special Olympics to discover who started it, its purpose, and the people it is helping. Research should include the local organization that sponsors the Special Olympics in your community and the athletes from your community who have participated.

3. When research has been completed, divide students into small groups. Have them identify professional athletes who have made a contribution to the Special Olympics and describe those accomplishments. Athletes can be local or national.

4. Invite a Special Olympian to speak to the class. Have him or her describe experiences while competing.

5. After meeting with the Special Olympian, students should create a display for the school highlighting the athletes and the organization. The display should include information about how students and others can support the organization by volunteering.

## ASSESSMENT

To evaluate students' work, use the Standards for Evaluating Work on page 59 of this booklet, along with Rubric 3: Artwork and Rubric 29: Presentations in the *Alternative Assessment Handbook* or in a customizable format on the One-Stop Planner.

# Planning Guidelines

In this activity, you will research the origins of the Special Olympics. You will begin by researching how and by whom the organization was founded and what purpose it was intended to serve. You should learn about the size and structure of the organization, how it is funded, and the similarities between it and the Olympics. Research should also include information about the local branch of the Special Olympics. Who takes part? How do athletes qualify to compete? Who runs it locally or sponsors it? When do the events occur and where in your community are they held? Contact the local office of the Special Olympics to arrange for a visitor from the organization and a Special Olympian to come to your class. Learn about the organization first-hand, what events the Olympian competed in, and how volunteers are utilized in the organization. After meeting with the visitors, you should create a display for your school describing the accomplishments of Special Olympians and providing information about the Special Olympics.

1. Start by researching the origins of the Special Olympics. Learn all you can from a variety of sources that discuss how the organization was founded and the primary organizers. Learn about the population it serves and how its medals are awarded. Also learn about what sports events it includes in its competitions and who can compete.

2. Research the local Special Olympics in your community. Find out who sponsors it and when its events are held. Research to discover whether there are any Special Olympians in your community. Invite either a Special Olympian or a representative of the organization, or both, to come speak to your class.

3. Prepare questions to ask the visitors about their personal experience with the Special Olympics. Learn about the organization from them and what it is like to compete in an event.

4. After meeting with the visitors, continue researching to discover who the Special Olympians are and present their highlights. Look for either local or national Olympians. Use a variety of sources, including biographies, newspaper articles, and other sources, to collect information about their accomplishments.

5. Prepare a display with your highlighted athletes and their accomplishments for your school. The display should be educational and informational as well as creative and interesting. It should invite people to volunteer to help the organization. Discuss the value of what you have learned with your class. Explain the importance of volunteering for all organizations that help the people in your community.

## Standards for Evaluating Work

### EXCELLENT

- Student has researched the Special Olympics using a variety of sources. Student has compiled information about the founding of the organization and its purpose. Student has identified the population it serves and has learned about the organizational structure.

- Student has researched the local office of the Special Olympics. Student has identified the representative of the organization and has learned how the Special Olympics operates within the community. Student has also developed questions for the visitor which help explain what the organization means to the disabled athlete.

- Student has created a display that is informative, interesting, and has many of the Special Olympians highlighted on it. Their accomplishments are highlighted with interesting data presented in a variety of ways that add to the overall appearance of the display.

### ACCEPTABLE

- Student has researched the Special Olympics using several sources. Student has information on its founding and the organizers and can discuss its purpose.

- Student has researched the local office of the Special Olympics and can identify a representative to speak to the class. Student can discuss the organization within the community. The questions for the guest speakers are adequate.

- Student has contributed to the display by offering athletes for inclusion. Student has researched the special contributors to the Special Olympics and has several different presentations.

### UNACCEPTABLE

- Student has not researched adequately the information about the Special Olympics. Student has used only a few sources in his or her research.

- Student has not discovered whether the Special Olympics has a local component. Student does not know what the local community has to offer athletes who wish to compete in the Special Olympics.

- Student has not contributed to the display by providing information on athletes to include. Student has not researched any athlete's accomplishments.

## Task Sheet

Check off the following tasks as you complete the activity.

❑ **1.** Research to discover what the Special Olympics is, how it operates, and who founded it. Also discover what its purpose is and the population it serves. Find out how many athletes participate and what sports are included.

❑ **2.** While you research, find out whether there is a local component of the Special Olympics that offers its services to members of your community. Who operates it? Who participates?

❑ **3.** Invite a representative of the local Special Olympics to come to your class. Also invite a Special Olympian to visit. Discuss their experiences with them. Write out the questions you want answered about how they compete and win medals.

❑ **4.** Research Special Olympic "heroes." Who are they, and what mark have they left on this organization? These can be either local or national. Describe what their accomplishments are while you research.

❑ **5.** Create a display for the Special Olympics to share with your school. Use the highlights of the Special Olympians whom you have researched. Include information about the organization. Be creative in your display, using several sources and different ways to present the material. Include information about how to volunteer for the Special Olympics and when the local events are held.

# Back away from Crime

## OBJECTIVES

After completing this activity, students will be able to:

- Identify the major sources of juvenile crime in their community.

- Identify organizations in their community that try to prevent juvenile crime.

- Discuss ways to advise juveniles of the consequences of crime.

## OVERVIEW

In this activity, students will contact their local police departments to learn about the major types of criminal conduct committed by juveniles in their community. Students will discuss creative ways to alert juveniles to stay out of trouble. Students will research to learn about the consequences of these particular crimes. Students will also identify places where juveniles frequently congregate, contact those businesses or organizations, and request that they be allowed to display posters warning juveniles of the consequences of these crimes. Students will then create posters depicting this information that will be placed at these local businesses or other sites. Students should also research local organizations working to prevent juvenile crime to determine whether they are effective.

## PLANNING

**Suggested Time** Plan to spend at least one 45-minute class period and two homework assignments on this activity.

**Resources** Students can contact the local police for information on crime statistics and local organizations that try to prevent juvenile crime. Students can contact local businesses juveniles frequent for permission to display their posters.

**Preparation** You may want to have students look at examples of crime-prevention posters for ideas and investigate crime prevention services available locally.

## IMPLEMENTATION

1. Discuss the project with the class. You might begin by discussing the types of crimes identified in the chapter and have the students guess what crimes occur most frequently in their community. Distribute copies of the Planning Guidelines, Standards for Evaluating Your Work, and Task Sheet to the class. Give the students a time frame for completing the project.

2. Have students contact the local law-enforcement agency. Ask about the top three or four types of crime committed by juveniles in your community. Have students find out how prevalent these crimes are. Divide the students into small groups. The number will depend on how many types of crimes are to be researched. Each group should focus on one crime.

3. When the crimes are identified, have students research the penalties for those crimes and the local organizations that try to prevent them. Then, have the students create posters advising juveniles about the crimes and the penalties. Have them be creative by using as many types of media as possible.

4. When groups have finished this task, have them contact local businesses and other sites that juveniles frequent. Ask the proprietors or others in authority to display the posters. The students should identify all types of businesses where juveniles are likely to commit these types of offenses. For example, shoplifters obviously target stores, but other types of crime may occur in skating rinks, playgrounds, eating establishments, and other businesses.

## ASSESSMENT

To evaluate students' work, use the Standards for Evaluating Work on page 63 of this booklet, along with Rubric 3: Artwork and Rubric 28: Posters in the *Alternative Assessment Handbook* or in a customizable format on the One-Stop Planner.

# Planning Guidelines

In this activity, you will be working in small groups to learn about the local juvenile crime rate. You will discuss with the local law-enforcement agency what crimes are committed most often in your community by juveniles, the penalties for those crimes, and the local organizations that try to prevent criminal conduct by juveniles. You will then discuss with those local agencies whether they are doing an effective job and their reasons for the crime rate in your community. Using this information, you will be assigned to a small group that will focus on one crime. Putting together all the information you learned, create a poster that advises juveniles of the crime you are targeting, the penalties for the crime, and how and why they should avoid such criminal conduct. Include the names of the crime-prevention organizations on the poster. Be creative. Think of what you would want to see on a poster that would make a difference to you. Then, after your posters are created, contact local businesses and other places where juveniles generally congregate and ask if your poster can be displayed. Think about all types of businesses and the crime you are covering. For example, if you are covering shoplifting, you want to target stores, but you may also contact skating rinks, bowling alleys, or other types of businesses where juveniles are likely to gather.

1. Before meeting with your small group, contact your local law-enforcement agency. Talk with them about the major types of crimes that juveniles commit in your community. You can focus on serious crimes or misdemeanors, but try to identify the leading crimes. Discuss with the police what they think could help prevent crimes and any crime-prevention organizations that address juvenile crime.

2. Contact the agencies that target juvenile crime prevention. Ask them to assess their effectiveness. Find out about the activities they sponsor that are directed toward preventing juveniles from getting into trouble. Find out what these agencies think is needed in your community.

3. In your small group, focus your ideas on what you have learned from the police and the agencies or organizations you've talked to. Create a poster designed to depict the crime, telling juveniles about the punishment for the crime, and other consequences of committing the crime. Present both the long-term and short-term consequences. For example, some crimes committed as juveniles may keep a person out of the military; committing other crimes may keep them from entering certain professions, such as the law.

4. Discuss with your group the businesses in your community where juveniles frequently congregate. Contact these businesses, describe what you have done, and offer to place your poster in their business establishment. Stress the purpose of the poster and your goals for creating it.

5. Discuss with the class what each of you can do to discourage juvenile crime.

# Standards for Evaluating Work

## EXCELLENT

• Student has participated fully in researching the crime statistics for the community. Student has contacted law-enforcement agencies, gathered data, and identified the major types of criminal conduct committed by juveniles. Student has also obtained information on the penalties for the crimes and has discussed short- and long-term consequences with law-enforcement representatives.

• Student has contacted crime-prevention agencies or organizations to discuss their effectiveness and has obtained information from them about what can be done to further discourage juvenile crime. Student understands the relationship between these organizations and crime prevention.

• Student has created a dynamic and interesting poster depicting the crime, its consequences, and ways to avoid it. The poster uses a mixture of media, is properly targeted to its audience, discusses the crime prevention organizations, and is effective in its purpose. Student has listed many businesses and other sites where the poster could be displayed.

## ACCEPTABLE

• Student has helped in contacting law-enforcement agencies and has gathered statistics necessary to identify the major crimes committed by juveniles in the community.

• Student has contacted the agencies or organizations and has discussed some of the ways the organizations prevent juvenile crime. Student does not fully understand the connection between prevention and juvenile crime.

• Student has done an adequate job creating a poster that depicts the crime and its consequences. Student is creative, includes relevant information about the agencies, and advises the juvenile how to stay out of trouble. Student makes suggestions about businesses where the poster could be displayed.

## UNACCEPTABLE

• Student has not contributed to the gathering of crime statistics for the community. Student has not interacted with law-enforcement agencies and does not understand the task.

• Student has not contacted any organization or agency involved with crime prevention. Student has not shown an understanding of the task nor of the connection between crime prevention and what these organizations do.

• Student has created a poster that poorly completes the task. The poster makes some effort to discuss the crime and its consequences, but does not do so in a creative way. Student fails to mention ways to stay out of trouble and does not discuss the agencies that help juveniles. Student has not contacted any businesses to get the poster displayed.

## Task Sheet

Check off the following tasks as you complete the activity.

☐ **1.** Contact the law-enforcement agency that handles crime in your community. It may be the sheriff's office or the police. Talk to its members about juvenile crime statistics in your community. Identify the top three or four crimes committed by juveniles in your area.

☐ **2.** While talking with the police, ask about organizations in your community that help deter juvenile crime. Get the police or sheriff's opinions about these organizations.

☐ **3.** In your small group, identify the crime to focus on. Research the penalties for this crime. Research the long-term and short-term consequences of committing this crime. How does the court system deal with a juvenile who commits this crime? What are the long-term implications of having a criminal record? What kinds of professions would a person be barred from entering if they have a juvenile criminal record?

☐ **4.** Talk to the organizations or agencies that you discovered in your community that try to prevent juvenile crime. What suggestions do they have on how to lessen or stop crime? What do they suggest are the main causes of crime in juveniles? How do these ideas compare with the suggestions given in your textbook?

☐ **5.** With your group, discuss what you have learned about the crime from all the resources you've contacted and researched. Create a poster that depicts the crime, its consequences if committed by a juvenile, the penalty for the crime, and the agencies or organizations that can help keep a juvenile out of trouble. Be creative in making your poster. Include unusual or original pictures or ideas that get the point across.

☐ **6.** With your group, think of local businesses or other sites in your community where juveniles often go. These can be stores or recreational businesses, such as skating rinks or bowling alleys. Contact these local businesses, explain what you have done and why you have done it, and ask whether you may display your poster in their business where juveniles can see it.

☐ **7.** Discuss with your class what you learned about the particular crimes you investigated. What were the penalties and what creative ways were suggested to prevent juveniles from committing these crimes?

# Who Wants To Be An Entrepreneur?

## OBJECTIVES

After completing this activity, students will be able to:

• Create a business plan for starting a business.

• Identify sources in the community for the supplies and materials needed for the business.

• Discuss the benefits and drawbacks of starting a business in their community.

## OVERVIEW

In this activity, students will think of a business they would like to start, develop a business plan, and identify sources in the community they could use for starting the business. They will develop a financial plan, determine the form of the business, identify a location for the business, and discuss the sources of labor, capital, and supplies for its operation. Students will invite a member of the banking or investment community to the class to review their business plans and give advice as to its feasibility. Students will interview business owners in their community to determine how they started their businesses and ask for advice about potential pitfalls the students may have overlooked.

## PLANNING

**Suggested Time** Plan to spend at least three 45-minute class periods and three homework assignments on this activity.

**Resources** Students can identify existing businesses from their community. Students can call the local Small Business Administration office or local bank for an adviser. Students can obtain instructions on preparing a business plan from the Internet.

**Preparation** You may want to obtain a sample balance sheet to assist with preparing the business plan. These are easily obtainable from the Internet. One site with easy instructions is: http://www.ameritrade.com/educationv2/fhtml/learning/ubalsheets.fhtml#balance.

## IMPLEMENTATION

1. Discuss the project with the class. Get them to suggest a business they want to start in their community. Using the textbook, have students identify the type of business entity that would work best for the business they wish to create. Distribute copies of the Planning Guidelines, Standards for Evaluating Your Work, and Task Sheet to the class. Give students a time frame for completing the project.

2. Students can work together as a class or can be placed in small groups to develop the business plan. Have the students obtain a sample financial planning sheet. Have them complete it by obtaining information about what they would need to start the business, e.g., money, supplies, labor, location, etc. Using this information, complete the business plan.

3. Invite a speaker from the Small Business Administration or an investment banker from your local bank to review the business plan and advise students as to its feasibility. Have the students discuss what else they need or whether their plan is realistic.

4. Have students locate business owners in their community. In small groups, have students interview the business owners to see how they started, what community services they have used to help them stay in business, and what advice they would give to someone thinking about starting a business in the community.

## ASSESSMENT

To evaluate students' work, use the Standards for Evaluating Work on page 67 of this booklet, along with Rubric 30: Research, and Rubric 35: Solving Problems, in the *Alternative Assessment Handbook* or in a customizable format on the One-Stop Planner.

# Planning Guidelines

In this activity, think of a type of business you want to see in your community and develop a business plan for it. Using a financial planning guide, you will determine what you need for the business and the resources in your community for supplying these needs. You will interact with a member of the investment community to assess the feasibility of your plan and to suggest ways to improve it. You will also seek advice from business owners in your community about the benefits and drawbacks of starting a business in your community and their personal experiences in running a business in your community.

1. Think of a business you would like to see in your community. This can be any kind of business, because it will only be created on paper. You might want to start a business that competes with one already in existence, such as a restaurant, or you might want to think of a new business that is not available in your town. An example might be a fresh fruit and ice cream stand that operates from a portable vendor, like the kind you see at amusement parks or fairs.

2. Obtain a financial planning guideline that you can use to help you think of all the financial aspects of operating a business. For example, you will have to determine your assets and liabilities; sources of capital for start up, such as obtaining the vending truck; and supplies to sell. You should identify all your needs and assets.

3. After determining what you will need, identify sources in your community that can supply those needs. Where will you operate? Who will work for you? Do you need a license to do business? How much will that cost? Where will you store supplies? For the ice cream/fruit vendor idea, how will you get a truck to move your machine?

4. After completing your business plan, invite a guest speaker to discuss with the class the feasibility of your business plan. A representative from the banking community who reviews business plans to determine if the bank is interested in financing the business, or a member of the Small Business Administration who reviews business plans to evaluate whether they qualify for government loans would be ideal. Discuss your business plan with your guest speaker and have him or her evaluate your plan.

5. Determine who the business owners are in your community. Interview the owners about how they started their businesses. Locate owners of corporations, companies, sole proprietorships, and partnerships, if possible. Find out what they went through when their business started. Get advice about starting a business in your community. Ask whether they took advantage of any local resources available to small businesses in your community, and if so, which ones and why. If you can locate the owner of a failed business, ask why the owner thinks it failed. Try to obtain as much information from these owners as you can so that you can avoid any pitfalls they may have dealt with.

# Standards for Evaluating Work

## EXCELLENT

- Student has participated fully in creating the business and the business plan. Student's business plan contains all the needed elements for starting a business and is well thought out and complete.

- Student has identified an appropriate person to invite to the class to discuss starting a business and to review the student's business plan. Student's questions for the guest are well thought out and designed to get thorough information to help implement the plan.

- Student has identified business owners in the community to interview. Student has obtained the names of owners of a variety of business entities, including corporations, partnerships, limited partnerships, and sole proprietorships. Student's interviews provide tremendous insight into starting a business in the community and the things to consider, other than the bottom line, in order to be successful.

## ACCEPTABLE

- Student has helped to create a business. Student's business plan is adequate but not thorough. Student has not thought out all the components needed to create a complete plan.

- Student has identified the appropriate person to invite to class to review and assess the business plan. Student's questions to the guest speaker are adequate but are not designed to get the business off the ground and to determine what is needed to improve the plan.

- Student has identified several business owners in the community. Student's interviews are good and give the student some insight into what it takes to run a business beyond financial assets. Student has identified business owners from a variety of business entities.

## UNACCEPTABLE

- Student has not contributed toward creating a business. Student has a poorly executed business plan and has not thought about all the components necessary to start a business.

- Student has not identified an appropriate person to speak to the class. Student has not formulated any questions designed to get the business off the ground nor to help assess the business plan and move it forward.

- Student has not identified very many owners to talk to about their business. Student has not identified owners from a variety of business entities. Student's interviews with the owners do not uncover information that would help a new business owner in this community.

## Chapter 17, Community Service and Participation Activity, continued

---

# Task Sheet

Check off the following tasks as you complete the activity.

❑ **1.** Create a business, along with your classmates, that you would like to see exist in your community. This can be a business that is brand new or one that competes with a business that already exists.

❑ **2.** After thinking of the business you want to create, obtain a financial planning guide to help you list the assets and liabilities of your business and identify what you will need to start your business. Identify all the sources in your community that can supply you with what you need. Use the textbook to help you think about what you will need for each component of your business.

❑ **3.** After you have created your plan, invite a member of the investment community to your class to review and assess the feasibility of your plan. This can be a member of the banking community, a lending institution, or the Small Business Administration.

❑ **4.** While listening to your guest speaker, think of questions that you can ask to help fill in the blanks of your plan. What does the speaker suggest that you need to do to get the business up and running? How would you obtain those things?

❑ **5.** Identify business owners in your community from a variety of business entities. Interview these owners for their advice on starting and keeping a business. Find out about their experiences in opening their businesses. What advice would they give you for starting a business in your community? Find out whether they ever used the services available in your community to help businesses. What were these services?

❑ **6.** Discuss with your class whether the business you created is actually feasible and what you would be willing to invest to make it happen. Discuss with them the drawbacks of being in business. How many of your classmates aspire to own their own businesses? Has this exercise encouraged or discouraged these aspirations? Why or why not?

---

# Where Does the Grocery Store Shop for Food?

## OBJECTIVES

After completing this activity, students will be able to:

- Identify the origin of products they use everyday.

- Discuss the movement of goods from around the world to their local markets.

- Determine how their local markets get supplies.

## OVERVIEW

In this activity, students will gather information about how their local grocery stores obtain the goods that they sell. Students will go to a local grocery store, choose a variety of items, and investigate the origins of the items. Students should choose from several food groups and examine labels for information about the items. After identifying the location of origin, which is usually printed on the label, students should trace exactly how the item got to the store. Students will need to investigate various countries around the world and find out how the items are made and transported to this country. Students will do the same for items made in the United States. The students will then use a world map to show the route these items took before landing in their local market.

## PLANNING

**Suggested Time** Plan to spend at least two 45-minute class periods and two homework assignments on this activity.

**Resources** Students can go to any local grocery store for this project. The store should carry a variety of items. Research into trade routes can be conducted on the Internet by visiting the Web sites of the producers or at the library.

**Preparation** You may want to peruse the grocery store for items from different countries. Suggest that students look for items that have both foreign and domestic origins. Have them look for locally produced items as well.

## IMPLEMENTATION

1. Discuss the project with the class. You might begin by having the students think of foreign foods that they like, or food that is out of season for your location but still available for purchase at the store. Ask them to consider the grocery store as a food representative of the world. Find out whether the students have any idea how food gets transported to the local store. Distribute copies of the Planning Guidelines, Standards for Evaluating Your Work, and Task Sheet to the class. Give the students a time frame for completing the project.

2. Have students identify foods from around the world, the United States, and local producers. This can be done on their next trip to the grocery store, or a special trip can be made for this purpose. After identifying the items, students should be divided into small groups of three or four and they should select several food items to investigate.

3. Students should research how the items they have chosen made their way from the point of origin to the local markets. Attention should be given to local production, transportation from the producing country, and transportation once in the United States.

4. When groups have finished this task, have them plot their items' movement from the point of origin to the local grocery store. A map of the world should be used to demonstrate this movement. Different transportation methods—land, air, and sea travel—and production methods should be distinguished on the map.

## ASSESSMENT

To evaluate students' work, use the Standards for Evaluating Work on page 71 of this booklet along with Rubric 1: Acquiring Information, and Rubric 20: Map Creation in the *Alternative Assessment Handbook* or in a customizable format on the One-Stop Planner.

# Planning Guidelines

In this activity, you will be working in small groups to learn how the local grocery store in your community gets its supplies from around the world. You will research the trade and transportation routes for some of the products that you use and enjoy. You also will learn about how these items are produced around the world. You might ask your local grocery store manager how items are selected for sale in the store and others are excluded. Try to find out whether most items in your grocery store are domestically produced or are imported from other countries. You will learn that to provide all the choices you have available for purchase requires a tremendous amount of logistical planning and work—all so you can just pick the item off the shelf. You might learn, too, that when something is unavailable, it is not always easy to replace.

1. Take a trip to the grocery store either on your own, with friends from class, or as a class trip. While there, look for items that you think might be imported from a foreign country, domestically produced, or locally produced. Write down what this item is and all the information about where it comes from that appears on the label. If the company that produced the item has a Web site, be sure to include that information. Do this for about 20 items.

2. Once back in class, combine your items with the ones found by everyone else in your group so that you all can choose a few of each kind of item. For example, make sure your group has selected some imported items, some domestically produced items, and some locally produced items.

3. Begin your research on the places where the items are made to see if you can determine exactly how and by whom the item was produced. For example, macadamia nuts were probably grown in Hawaii, canned there, and then sent to the mainland United States via plane or ship. Then, they were probably sent by truck or rail to some nearby distribution center, then delivered to your local grocer's warehouse by truck, and then finally to your local grocery store. Trace the route and method of production as much as you can for each item.

4. Once all the items have been charted for your group, work with the rest of the class to create a map that identifies all the different points of origin for items in your grocery store. Identify in creative ways how the items were produced using icons that represent that way. For example, use one icon for farming, one for dairy, etc. Do the same for methods of transportation.

5. After creating your map, discuss with the class how your grocery store is really a "micro" world market. How many of you thought about where and how goods were obtained before this exercise? How would you go about marketing your product to the world if you began to produce an item? How do you think the small farmers in foreign countries got involved in the global market? How would you?

# Standards for Evaluating Work

## EXCELLENT

• Student has obtained a comprehensive list of items that is representative of many possible markets. The list includes different types of foods from different parts of the world.

• Student has researched the methods of production for the items on his or her list and can describe the methods of collection and transportation throughout the entire process.

• Student has contributed to the map of the world's suppliers of the local grocery store. Student's icons are imaginative and represent the method of production and the method of transportation used to gather the items. Student has used a variety of grocery items from a wide variety of sources.

## ACCEPTABLE

• Student has created a list of items from foreign, domestic, and local markets. Student has some possibilities of each kind of item needed to adequately do the exercise.

• Student has collected some information on the methods of processing the items and has some information about the transportation methods used to get goods from the point of origin to the local store.

• Student has contributed to the map of the world and has identified several points of origin for the local grocery supplies. Student has represented the method of production and transportation imaginatively.

## UNACCEPTABLE

• Student has only a few items or the items do not represent the foreign, domestic, and local markets.

• Student has little information showing how items are processed and transported from local markets to the grocery store.

• Student has not contributed very much to the map of the world and has identified only a few items and their points of origin in the world. Student has not clearly identified the methods of production or transportation used in his or her items.

Name _____ Class _____ Date _____

# Task Sheet

Check off the following tasks as you complete the activity.

❏ **1.** Obtain a list of food items from around the world that are stocked on your grocery store shelves. Write down the name of the item and everything you can learn from the label about where and how that item is produced. You will need about 20 items. Get at least a few items each from foreign sources, domestic sources, and local sources.

❏ **2.** After compiling the list, compare your list with the lists of other students. Divide the items into the three categories (foreign, domestic, and local). Divide the class into small groups. Each group should take several items from each of the three categories to investigate.

❏ **3.** Research the items that you have chosen or are assigned. You should find out how the item is produced, where exactly in the world it is produced, and how it is shipped from its point of origin to your local grocery store. Pay special attention to shipping routes and the method of transportation used.

❏ **4.** After finishing your research, get a large map of the world. Using each item, plot out its point of origin, identify the method of production, and then plot the transportation route and method of travel it followed to get from its original location to your grocery store. If necessary, create a legend for your map, identifying specific or unique information.

❏ **5.** Have a class discussion about your map of the world and how many items come from around the world. Discuss how significant it is to have the kinds of choices that a typical grocery store gives each of its customers. Discuss the benefits of having local producers versus foreign imports and vice versa. How would you go about marketing a product to the world if you produced some food item? How are you part of the global market?

# The Hidden Costs of Owning a Home

## OBJECTIVES

After completing this activity, students will be able to:

- Identify the major lending institutions in their community.

- Describe and compare the types of services they provide to their customers.

- Determine the best lender for financing their first home purchase.

## OVERVIEW

In this activity, students will examine the costs of home ownership. They will be given a work and credit history, an amount of money to put down on the purchase of a home, and a list of houses available for purchase in their community. Students will research lending institutions, compare lending rates, and apply to purchase a home using their given history. Students will calculate the true cost of home ownership, including insurance, closing costs, points, and the difference between fixed and adjustable mortgage rates and 15-, 20-, and 30-year mortgages. Students will contact insurance companies to learn the costs of insurance for homeowners in their communities. Students also will research their communities to determine whether there are any first-time buyers' rates, empowerment zones, or other programs that make purchasing a home more affordable.

## PLANNING

**Suggested Time** Plan to spend at least two 45-minute class periods and two homework assignments on this activity.

**Resources** Students can locate their lending institutions using the Yellow Pages.

**Preparation** You may want to prepare one or more credit and work histories for the class to use. You may also contact a real estate agent for prequalification forms and a list of houses available in the market. You may also identify a banker to review the students' applications.

## IMPLEMENTATION

1. Discuss the project with the class. You might begin by asking students whether there are any homes for sale in their neighborhoods and whether they know how to purchase a home. Distribute copies of the Planning Guidelines, Standards for Evaluating Your Work, and Task Sheet to the class. Give students a time frame for completing the project.

2. Provide students with a work and credit history and pre-qualification forms to determine their price range for buying a home. Have students contact all the major lending institutions in the community and secure forms for applying for a mortgage. Students should learn the mortgage rates and the list of services provided by each institution.

3. Students should research all aspects of purchasing a home, including any hidden costs such as closing costs, points, insurance, and any other costs associated with buying and owning a home. Students should calculate the difference in total costs for different types of mortgages and different durations. Students can work in small groups or as a class for this exercise.

4. When all calculations are complete, have students research whether there are any special offers for special groups, e.g., veterans, first-time buyers, empowerment-zone purchases, etc. Have students determine what it takes to qualify for such programs and the incentives offered by these programs.

## ASSESSMENT

To evaluate students' work, use the Standards for Evaluating Work on page 11 of this booklet, along with Rubric 1: Acquiring Information and Rubric 9: Comparing and Contrasting in the *Alternative Assessment Handbook* or in a customizable format on the One-Stop Planner.

# Planning Guidelines

In this activity, you will learn about purchasing a home for your family. You will begin by researching all the major lending institutions in your community to determine their lending rates and policies. You will learn about the different types of mortgages available, about any special deals in your community to make purchasing a home for the first time easier, and whether certain parts of your community are targeted for special rates or deals if a home is purchased there. You also will research the hidden or unexpected costs associated with home buying, such as insurance and closing costs. You will find out what property is available for purchase in your community and what homes you are qualified financially to buy. To do this, a work and credit history will be given to you by your teacher. You will have to locate property and, using application forms from the lending institutions you have identified, apply for a loan to purchase the home. Calculate the total cost of purchasing your home, using all the data you have gathered from all the sources you have specified.

1. Contact or visit the major lending institutions in your community. Inquire about their lending rates and bank services for their customers. Obtain an application for purchasing a home from them.

2. After you obtain a work and credit history for your group or class, research the available properties for sale in your community or in one area of your community. Determine by completing a prequalification form (that you have obtained from the lending institution) the amount that you can afford to pay for a house. Locate houses within your price range and complete the prequalification form for this purchase.

3. Using the local lending rates and the terms of your mortgage agreement, determine exactly how much your house will cost you over the life of your mortgage.

4. Calculate the cost of obtaining insurance to protect your home and its contents. What other costs are associated with purchasing a home? Include these costs in your total price.

5. Research your community to determine whether there are any first-time buyers' programs or discount mortgages you can benefit from. Are there any benefits that you qualify for, such as veteran's benefits? Are you willing to purchase your home in a neighborhood such as an empowerment zone or high-risk area if it means getting a significant deduction in taxes or mortgage rates?

6. Discuss with your class the benefits of home ownership. Why is owning a home such a big part of the American dream? What are some of the financial benefits for owning rather than renting your home? What nonfinancial considerations do you think go into purchasing a home?

# Standards for Evaluating Work

## EXCELLENT

- Student has researched the lending institutions in the community and has learned what services the institution offers its customers. Student has compared the rates and knows which institution has the best to offer.

- Student has calculated the costs of purchasing a home and has included all the hidden and unexpected costs. Student has completed an application for a home mortgage and has included all items needed from the work and credit history provided by the teacher. Student has researched the available homes in the community and has prequalified for financing.

- Student has researched the community and can identify the discount programs offered to first-time buyers and others who qualify under the specific plans. Student can discuss the empowerment zones and other areas in the community that offer discounts for homebuyers. Student can discuss how to qualify for these homes.

## ACCEPTABLE

- Student has researched the lending institutions in the community. Student has gathered information about the types of services they offer.

- Student has calculated the costs of purchasing a home using the information obtained from the bank. Student has completed the application for a home mortgage. Student has prequalified for financing and has researched available homes in the community.

- Student has researched and found several discount programs offered to first-time buyers. Student can discuss some of the discount plans available in the community and describe how to qualify under the programs.

## UNACCEPTABLE

- Student has researched a few lending institutions but has not done a complete survey of the services offered at each one.

- Student has used some of the information obtained from the lending institution to prepare an application but has not calculated the cost of purchasing the house. Student has not pre-qualified for financing, nor has he or she researched the homes in the community available to purchase.

- Student has researched some of the programs offered to first-time buyers but cannot describe the programs or how to qualify for their benefits.

Name _____ Class _____ Date _____

# Task Sheet

Check off the following tasks as you complete the activity.

❑ **1.** Obtain the names of the lending institutions in your community. Inquire about the services they offer to home buyers and their mortgage rates. Obtain a prequalification form and an application for purchasing a home.

❑ **2.** Obtain the work and credit history from your teacher to use to calculate how much you can afford to pay for your house. Using the forms you obtained from the lending institutions you contacted, prequalify for financing.

❑ **3.** Research your community or an area within your community and find out which homes are available to purchase. Determine which homes you qualify for using your prequalifying form.

❑ **4.** Complete an application for financing. Calculate the total costs of purchasing your home using the variables you received from the bank. For example, how much are you paying for your home if you have a fixed-rate mortgage for 15 years? For 30 years? What about an adjustable-rate mortgage?

❑ **5.** Using your research skills, find out whether there are any discount programs in your area that offer incentives to home buyers. What are the qualifications for taking advantage of these discounts? Would you be willing to do what is necessary to take advantage of such a deal? Why or why not?

# Recording History

## OBJECTIVES

After completing this activity, students will be able to:

- Describe the Great Depression's effects on their community.

- Discuss the ways people in their community coped with the Great Depression.

- Create an audio or visual history of their community.

## OVERVIEW

In this activity, students will learn about the people in their community who lived through the Great Depression. Students will conduct interviews with elders, learning about what happened to them during that time in America, and discover what effects the Great Depression had on their community as a whole. Students will locate octogenarians through family ties and visits to nursing homes or other communities of the elderly and learn the individual stories of how they lived, worked, fed themselves or their families, etc. Students will create a video or audio record of their interviews and compile these recordings into a comprehensive history of their community during the Great Depression. Students will narrate or augment the video or audio with historical facts about their community that reinforce the stories told by these elders.

## PLANNING

**Suggested Time** Plan to spend at least two 45-minute class periods and three homework assignments on this activity. Students will also conduct an interview for this assignment.

**Resources** Students can use any person for the interview who can share information. Students can use the local library for historical information about their community.

**Preparation** You may want to determine whether any senior centers or assisted-living residences in your vicinity would be willing to participate in the project. You may also need to secure audio or video equipment.

## IMPLEMENTATION

1. Discuss the project with the class. You might begin by asking them what they would do if suddenly their family had no money because of economic conditions. Distribute copies of the Planning Guidelines, Standards for Evaluating Your Work, and Task Sheet to the class. Give the students a time frame for completing the project.

2. Tell students whether they will be creating an audio or video recording of their interviews. Have students locate an octogenarian to interview. Have them record the interview using audio or video equipment. Have students come up with a list of questions to ask each person interviewed so the student can obtain a chronicle of similar information to compare.

3. Have students research how their community reacted during the Great Depression. Find out whether banks failed, businesses closed, etc. Research should be correlated to the types of questions asked of the elders who are interviewed.

4. When the research and interviews are complete, students should complete an audiotape or video. If an audiotape is made, students should include their interviews, Depression-era music, and their own narrative describing other information they learned from their research. If a video is produced, students should include their interviews, music, photos, and other information they learned about their community.

## ASSESSMENT

To evaluate students' work, use the Standards for Evaluating Work on page 79 of this booklet, along with Rubric 4: Biographies, Rubric 18: Listening, and Rubric 22: Multimedia Presentations, in the *Alternative Assessment Handbook* or in a customizable format on the One-Stop Planner.

# Planning Guidelines

In this activity, you will create an audiotape or videotape that records a history of your community during the Great Depression. You will gather information about your community during that time by researching the archives of the public library. Look for photographs, newspaper accounts, and other primary-source documents that describe the events of the day. Next, locate an elder member of your community who can describe his or her personal experiences of living through the Great Depression. Try to locate someone who lived in your community during that time. Ask the person to describe his or her memories of surviving during the era. Record the conversation you have with this person using either a tape recorder or video recorder. If you are creating an audiotape, augment your audio recording with Depression-era music and your own narration in between the interviews. If you are creating a videotape, highlight your tape with photos of your community during the Great Depression, appropriate music, and your interviews.

1. Discuss the project with your classmates. Determine what information you want to obtain in your interviews that would help you understand how your community fared during the Great Depression. If your community did not exist, do a more general search using a specific region of your state. Determine whether you will be creating an audiotape or videotape.

2. Research in your local library to gather background information about your community during the Great Depression. Find out whether there were bank or business failures, whether there were severe job shortages, or any other information that was documented from that time.

3. Locate an elder who lived in your community during the Great Depression to talk with. Begin the conversation by asking about the person generally and establish the person's ties to your community. You might then ask the questions you and your classmates have developed. Be sure to ask the interviewee for permission to use his or her information and name in whatever final program you are creating. Get the permission in writing.

4. When you have completed the research and interviews, the class should decide which interviews to use after listening to each one. It is not necessary to use them all, but a good cross-section of the community should be represented. For example, be sure to include owners of businesses and workers, minorities, women, and others who can add a diverse view. Decide who will narrate and what other information will be included. Be creative.

5. Put your audiotape or videotape together. Listen to it or watch it together as a class. Does it reflect the history that you researched? Are the portrayals of your community by the people you interviewed consistent with what you read or thought after you read the history? What accounts for the differences, if any? What important information did you learn about how your community responded during this era?

# Standards for Evaluating Work

## EXCELLENT

• Student has researched the background information of the community during the Great Depression and has obtained much useful information. Student has many different sources of material that describe life in the community during this time.

• Student has created thorough questions to ask the interviewees about life for them during the Great Depression. Student has located a suitable interviewee and has conducted the interview consistent with the task. Student has also gathered additional information from the interviewee to assist in completing the project.

• Student has done an excellent job with the audiotape or videotape. Student has put in creative touches that make the history complete and interesting.

## ACCEPTABLE

• Student has researched some background information about life in the community during the Great Depression. Student has a few different sources that can be used to describe the community during this time period.

• Student has formulated good questions to ask the interviewee that will give insight into life during the Great Depression. Student has located an interviewee and has done an adequate job of conducting the interview.

• Student has done an adequate job with the audiotape or videotape. Student has contributed to the project and added to its thoroughness in representing the community.

## UNACCEPTABLE

• Student has not done a thorough job researching the community and only has a few entries about the Great Depression and the community.

• Student has created some questions, but they are not especially well written nor are they designed to gather the type of information sought. Student has located an interviewee, but has not done a good job with the interview.

• Student has not contributed much to the audiotape or videotape that adds to the history of the community during this era. Student had no information to add other than the interview.

Name _____ Class _____ Date _____

## Task Sheet

Check off the following tasks as you complete the activity.

❑ **1.** Research information in the local library about your community during the Great Depression. Utilize all sources, including books, newspapers, photographs, business reports, and any other media to find out what life was like for your community during this time.

❑ **2.** While you research, pay special attention to businesses or buildings that still exist. Note the changes in the structures or institutions.

❑ **3.** Locate an older citizen in your community to interview about his or her life during this period. You may contact family members or friends or ask at a senior center or residential facility whether there are people who would be willing to talk to you about their lives during this time. When interviewing the people, be sure to get their permission in writing to use their names or stories in your audiotape or videotape.

❑ **4.** After all research and interviews are complete, decide whose interviews will be used in creating your history. Include a diverse representation of your community that includes people from all backgrounds and experiences.

❑ **5.** Decide what additional information from your research you will include as narration, music, or photos, and identify any additional information needed. Decide who will narrate the tape.

❑ **6.** Create your video or audio history. Watch or listen to it together as a class.

## The U.S. Economy and the World

# The Union Fight Over NAFTA

## OBJECTIVES

After completing this activity, students will be able to:

- Identify the local unions in their community.

- Discuss the positions that the unions took on the NAFTA agreement.

- Describe the positive and negative effects that NAFTA had on the local economy.

## OVERVIEW

In this activity, students will assess the effects that the North American Free Trade Agreement (NAFTA) has had on their community. Students will contact local union leaders and invite them to address the class to talk about their positions on NAFTA. Students will research why unions generally opposed NAFTA and what they feared would happen after it was passed. After meeting with union leaders and researching the effects NAFTA has had since its signing in 1993, students will discuss the position of the unions and decide for themselves whether the agreement was a good or bad thing for the U.S. economy. Students will create a FAQs (Frequently Asked Questions) booklet describing their findings about NAFTA and whether it has had positive or negative effects on their community.

## PLANNING

**Suggested Time** Plan to spend at least two 45-minute class periods and two homework assignments on this activity.

**Resources** Students can find their local unions through the library or Yellow Pages. Students may research the effects of NAFTA at the library or on the Internet.

**Preparation** Contact local union representatives to make arrangements for speakers.

## IMPLEMENTATION

1. Discuss the project with the class. You can ask students whether they understand the relationship between labor costs and the price paid for goods. You might also ask whether they think free trade between Mexico, Canada, and the United States is a good thing. Distribute copies of the Planning Guidelines, Standards for Evaluating Your Work, and Task Sheet to the class. Give the students a time frame for completing the project.

2. Have the students locate unions in the community. Have them contact these unions and ask them about their positions on NAFTA while it was debated in Congress and whether their positions have changed since it went into effect in 1993. Ask whether the unions have members who can discuss their positions with the class. Then have them research the amount of money NAFTA trade has contributed to the U.S. economy.

3. Divide the class into small groups. Have the students research the pros and cons of NAFTA. Have them identify the main arguments for and against its passage. Have them write questions to ask the speakers about what the unions did to prevent or help its passage. Students should also draw their own conclusions about NAFTA based on the unions' positions and their own research.

4. Have students create a booklet of FAQs about NAFTA. If there were questions from the community about the effects of NAFTA on the local or national economy, what information could the student share?

## ASSESSMENT

To evaluate students' work, use the Standards for Evaluating Work on page 83 of this booklet, along with Rubric 9: Comparing and Contrasting and Rubric 16: Judging Information in the *Alternative Assessment Handbook* or in a customizable format on the One-Stop Planner.

# Planning Guidelines

In this activity, you will be working in small groups to learn about the effect of the North American Free Trade Agreement (NAFTA) on your local economy. By talking to local union representatives, you will find out what unions thought about NAFTA and whether they supported its passage. You will also research NAFTA in your library or on the Internet to discover why its proponents favored it and what it has done for the economy. Use a variety of sources to gather information. Invite the union leaders to speak to your class. Then, you can prepare a booklet called *FAQs about NAFTA* to help people learn about the real effects of this agreement both nationally and locally.

1. Identify the local unions in your community. Contact them to discover what their positions were on NAFTA as it waas being debated. Invite them to speak to your class on the subject.

2. Research NAFTA. Find out why some people supported its passage. Find out why its opponents thought it would hurt the country. Take good notes and try to group the reasons into categories. Use as many sources as possible. Finally, find out who voted for and against the passage of NAFTA in Congress.

3. In your small group, try to think of questions based on your research to ask the union representatives. Why were they for or against NAFTA? What specifically did they think would happen?

4. After talking to your group, completing your research, and listening to the union speakers, answer the questions most frequently asked about the effects of NAFTA on the economy nationally and locally. Did the bad (or good) things that were predicted about this agreement actually occur? Who was right or wrong about it?

5. Put your questions and answers about NAFTA in a Frequently Asked Questions (FAQs) booklet that can be used to educate people about NAFTA. Try to address the questions that people had about its advantages and disadvantages.

# Standards for Evaluating Work

## EXCELLENT

- Student has researched the arguments for and against on the passage of NAFTA. Student has accumulated many facts from many sources that clearly identify the proponents' and opponents' positions.

- Student has worked hard in the small group to come up with questions that are challenging to the union representatives and helped answer questions about the effects of NAFTA on the local economy.

- Student has participated fully in the creation of the booklet. Student has identified the FAQs about NAFTA and has answered them in concise and accurate ways. Student has done an excellent job of gathering information on the national and local effects of NAFTA.

## ACCEPTABLE

- Student has researched some of the arguments that were used in the NAFTA debate. Student can identify a good number of arguments for and against the measure.

- Student has done a fair amount of work in the small group to come up with questions for the union representatives.

- Student has participated in the creation of the booklet. Student has been able to provide answers for the most frequently asked questions about NAFTA and has contributed to the booklet. Student has gathered information about the effects of NAFTA on the national and local economies.

## UNACCEPTABLE

- Student has done some research on the NAFTA debate but has used only a few sources and can identify only a few arguments.

- Student has not helped the small groups come up with questions that probe the unions' position on NAFTA. Student's questions do not help to identify or address the issues.

- Student has not been able to contribute to the booklet because the information gathered in his or her research is inadequate. Student has not been able to address questions and answers about the effects of NAFTA on the local and national economies.

# Task Sheet

Check off the following tasks as you complete them.

❑ **1.** Find out which unions operate in your community. Contact the unions and invite union representatives to come speak to your class about the unions' position on NAFTA.

❑ **2.** Use the library or the Internet to research the arguments for and against the passage of NAFTA. Identify the debates. Identify the arguments for and against NAFTA and who was on each side.

❑ **3.** In your small groups, try to formulate questions that address the arguments that you found in your research.

❑ **4.** After meeting with the union representatives, in your small groups consider the pros and cons of NAFTA that you originally found in your research. Have the things that the opponents warned about actually happened? Have those predictions come true in your community? Nationally? Have the good things that the proponents anticipated happened? Have they happened in your community? Nationally?

❑ **5.** Create a booklet called *FAQs about NAFTA*. In it, answer the questions that people had about the results of NAFTA's passage. Address the concerns of both sides.

# Marketing Yourself

## OBJECTIVES

After completing this activity, students will be able to:

- Identify characteristics that make them attractive for employment, higher education, or the military.
- Recognize the importance of self-assessment.
- Create a resume that can be used for selling themselves on any application.

## OVERVIEW

In this activity, students will complete an application for employment, college, and the military using a resume that they have created. Students will create a resume by evaluating their skills, academic careers, and outside activities. They should determine what they need to accomplish in their remaining school years to meet their ultimate professional goals. Students will obtain a job application from any employer likely to hire unskilled labor, an online college application, and information on enlisting in the military from the local recruitment office. Students will complete their resume using the information in the textbook to identify their marketable skills for each type of application.

## PLANNING

**Suggested Time** Plan to spend at least two 45-minute class periods and one homework assignment on this activity.

**Resources** Students can use any research tool, such as the Internet or the want ads, to find a job in the community. Students can visit a local recruitment office or go to the U.S. Armed Forces Web sites for information about military careers. Students can download a college application from the Internet.

**Preparation** You may want to provide students with a standard resume form to use or provide samples of different resumes and let them choose. These are readily available from the Internet, or your guidance office may have them.

## IMPLEMENTATION

1. Discuss the project with the class. You might begin by asking students to think of themselves as a product that they have to market. Ask them to think of their skills and attributes as selling points for the purpose of creating a resume of their lives. Distribute copies of the Planning Guidelines, Standards for Evaluating Your Work, and Task Sheet to the class. Give the students a time frame for completing the project.

2. Have students select a resume form to use. Students should categorize their information into the typical topics that are included in a resume, such as education, work experience, etc. Students should also consider other skills and outside activities, such as those mentioned in the text, to create additional categories to convey other important information about themselves.

3. When the resume is completed, have students obtain a job application from an employer of their choice, a college application from a college of their choice, and information about enlisting in the military branch of their choice.

4. Have each student complete each of these applications using the information contained in his or her resume. Have them assess their preparation for each of these opportunities. Have them discuss what education and experience they need to obtain to maximize their chances of getting the job, being accepted by the college, or succeeding in a military career.

## ASSESSMENT

To evaluate students' work, use the Standards for Evaluating Work on page 87 of this booklet, along with Rubric 30: Research, and Rubric 31: Resumes, in the *Alternative Assessment Handbook* or in a customizable format on the One-Stop Planner.

# Planning Guidelines

In this activity, you will create a resume. In this case, your resume will be used as a marketing tool to sell your skills and experience to a potential employer, college, or military recruiter. You will create your resume using the traditional categories of education and experience, but you will also perform a self-assessment of your other characteristics that might interest an employer, college, or the military. In evaluating yourself, think about the skills you have developed through hobbies or extracurricular activities. If you have a special aptitude for doing unusual things, how can those be translated into a marketable skill? Are you knowledgeable about anything in particular? Are you computer literate? Can you speak a foreign language? Are you artistic? Are you a problem-solver? Think about yourself in terms of what someone else might be looking for. In completing the applications, notice the kind of information asked about you. What are some things you can do to improve your chances of being offered the job, college, or military assignment of your choice when you graduate?

1. Obtain a resume form from your teacher. Use this form as a sample for creating your resume.

2. Using the textbook as a starting point, complete the resume. Include all the information about your education and experience. Include information about different schools you may have attended; the curriculum you studied; special courses you may have taken over your summer breaks; any job you have held, such as baby-sitting or working in a family business; and anything else that qualifies as education or experience.

3. Think about your extracurricular activities, hobbies, special abilities, and knowledge. Identify the skills you use in performing those things. For example, if you do volunteer work, what specifically do you do? List those experiences in the appropriate sections of your resume.

4. Obtain applications from three sources: one for a job you would like to have, one from a college you would like to attend, and one for a branch of the military you would consider. You can obtain information about the military from local recruitment offices. Complete all three applications by using your resume.

5. Assess your applications. What do you need to accomplish to be more competitive? What skills did they ask for that you are lacking? What educational requirements are listed on these applications? Do you meet them, or do you expect to before graduating? How appealing do you think you are currently to the employer, college, or military branch that you chose? What can you do to put yourself in a better position between now and the time you graduate?

# Standards for Evaluating Work

## EXCELLENT

- Student has created a resume that accurately and persuasively demonstrates marketable skills they acquired through their education and experiences. Student has placed his or her achievements in a positive light, highlighting academic skills and employment or related experiences.

- Student has done a self-assessment that is accurate. Student has identified qualities and translated them into skills that are highly sought and make him or her desirable to an employer or other entity.

- Student has obtained applications from all three sources. Student has completed the applications using the information from his or her resume and has identified other things necessary to make him or herself more competitive on all three applications, and provided ways to achieve those things.

## ACCEPTABLE

- Student has created a resume that accurately lists marketable skills they acquired through their education and experiences. Student has highlighted his or her academic and work experiences.

- Student has done a self-assessment that reflects some of his or her characteristics. Student has not been able to accurately translate those qualities into marketable skills.

- Student has obtained applications from all three sources. Student has completed the applications and has identified some of his or her shortcomings. Student has identified a few ways he or she can become more competitive.

## UNACCEPTABLE

- Student has not created a resume that lists marketable skills he or she acquired through education and experiences. Student has not understood the task of selling oneself in these areas.

- Student has not completed a self-assessment or identified any quality that translates into a marketable skill.

- Student has not obtained all three applications or has not completed those applications. Student has not been able to identify his or her shortcomings based on the applications and has not provided ways to meet the requirements of the job, college, or military service.

# Task Sheet

Check off the following tasks as you complete them.

❑ **1.** Obtain a sample resume from your teacher.

❑ **2.** Prepare the parts of the resume that include your education and experience. Be sure to include your curriculum from school and classes that you might have taken during the summer or outside of school. Include all your work experiences, such as baby-sitting jobs, work in the family business, or any work for neighbors or friends that you may have done.

❑ **3.** In another part of your resume, include other pertinent information about yourself. Perform a self-assessment of your marketable skills, using your other experiences as a guide. For example, if you have been a Boy Scout or Girl Scout, is there any skill you learned or performed that you can translate into a marketable skill to put on your resume? Did you hold an office in an organization? Does your family speak a language other than English at home? Are you fluent in that language? Have you been a camp counselor? Do you have a leadership role in your community? Have you volunteered for an organization? What did you do for them? What quality sets you apart from other students in your class or school? How can you describe that as a positive quality on your resume?

❑ **4.** Obtain an application from an employer you would like to work for, a college you would like to attend, and a branch of the military you would consider enlisting in (even if you have no intention currently of seeking a job, attending college, or enlisting in the military when you finish school). Complete these three applications thoroughly, using the information you have collected on your resume.

❑ **5.** After completing the applications, assess your qualifications for each of them. Do you feel qualified? What do you need to do to become competitive? Can you accomplish those things in the time you have left in school? What do you need to do to reach your goals?

# UN Security Council

## OBJECTIVES

After completing this activity, students will be able to:

- Examine the United Nations Security Council's function in light of September 11, 2001.
- Describe the significance of Security Council Resolution 1373.
- Discuss the way UN Resolution 1373 has impacted the community since September 11.

## OVERVIEW

In this activity, students will examine the UN Security Council and its role after the terrorist attacks on September 11, 2001. Students should research what measures the Security Council has taken to make the world safe and free from terrorism. Students should discover what the Security Council has required of its member nations and what resolutions it has adopted concerning terrorism. Students will examine Resolution 1373 and see that there are links between terrorism and crimes such as money laundering and illegal arms trafficking. Students should contact local banks or brokerage houses to see what specific reporting changes were required as a result of the Resolution. They should also contact law-enforcement agencies to see how these changes have been enforced. Students should then write a letter to their classmates describing what they learned about Resolution 1373.

## PLANNING

**Suggested Time** Plan to spend at least two 45-minute class periods and two homework assignments on this activity.

**Resources** Students can use the United Nations web site at *www.un.org* to access Security Council Resolution 1373.

**Preparation** You may want to print a copy of the four-page Resolution. Students can invite a banker, broker, and law-enforcement agent to visit the class to discuss the new regulations.

## IMPLEMENTATION

1. Discuss the project with the class. Get the students to focus on the chapter's discussion of the duties and functions of the United Nations. Have students talk about what it means to be peacekeepers and discuss why five specific countries are permanent members of the Security Council. Distribute copies of the Planning Guidelines, Standards for Evaluating Your Work, and Task Sheet to the class. Give the students a time frame for completing the project. To get to the document on the UN web site, click on Welcome, then UN Action Against Terrorism, then Security Council, then S/RES/1373(2001).

2. Divide the students into small groups. Read the resolution and have the students think about the far-reaching implications of what the resolution requires of each member nation. Have students discuss the connection the resolution makes between crime and terrorism.

3. Students should invite a speaker from a bank, a brokerage firm, or a law enforcement agency to speak to the class. The speaker should be knowledgeable about changes imposed by the resolution.

4. Have students think about the role that banks and other financial institutions now play in stopping terrorism. Have them evaluate the Resolution's goals. Students should write a letter to their classmates explaining the Resolution and how criminal acts are linked to terrorism.

## ASSESSMENT

To evaluate students' work, use the Standards for Evaluating Work on page 91 of this booklet, along with Rubric 17: Letters to Editors, and Rubric 41: Writing to Express in the *Alternative Assessment Handbook,* or in a customizable format on the One-Stop Planner.

# Planning Guidelines

In this activity, you will be working in small groups to discuss the role of the United Nations Security Council. Using the UN web site, you can learn about the primary resolution enacted by the UN since the terrorist acts of September 11, 2001—Resolution 1373. UN Security Council Resolution 1373 places responsibility on each of its members to fight terrorism by reporting certain criminal activity to law enforcement. Part of the resolution is aimed at dismantling the financial structure that supports terrorist groups. As a result, banks and other financial institutions now have increased responsibility in reporting certain criminal activity to law enforcement. Invite a member of a financial institution, such as a banker or broker, to speak to your class about the new rules that the Security Council Resolution 1373 imposes on them. Research the resolution and ask about the specific language that links criminal activity to terrorist groups. Discuss with the banker or broker how they see the ties among these activities. Learn how the UN really has a say in the daily activities and lives of people around the world.

1. Before meeting with your small group, research the UN Security Council. Discover the function and makeup of the Council and why it uses a structure of five permanent members and ten elected, two-term members. Who was on the Security Council on September 11, 2001?

2. In your small group, access the UN Security Council Resolution 1373 by going to the UN web site at *www.un.org*. What does the resolution say? What are its goals? What burden does it place on UN members? What major threats does it address? How does it connect illegal drugs, money, and terrorist activity?

3. Invite members of banking or other financial institutions to speak to your class, as well as a representative from a law-enforcement agency. Ask the financial representatives about their reporting requirements. What happens to the reports once they are made to law enforcement? How are innocent people protected?

4. In your small groups, draft a letter to your classmates explaining why there is a connection between crime and terrorism. Try to explain Resolution 1373 in terms your classmates understand. Describe how the resolution may help rid the world of terrorism. Describe how the fight against terrorism is global, involving all member nations of the United Nations.

5. Discuss with your class what you have learned and what you think of Resolution 1373. Also discuss whether you think Resolution 1373 would have been accepted by the UN before September 11, 2001.

# Standards for Evaluating Work

## EXCELLENT

- Student has researched the UN Security Council and can fully describe its functions and structure. Student has evaluated Resolution 1373 fully and can articulate its goals and purpose as well as its implementation.

- Student has contacted the proper personnel at a bank, brokerage house, or law enforcement agencies. Student has discussed with the small group the information needed to understand why there is a connection between criminal activity and terrorism. Student's questions to the speakers add to the understanding of the issues.

- Student has added a lot of information in the letter to his classmates explaining Resolution 1373, its purposes, and goals.

## ACCEPTABLE

- Student has researched the UN Security Council and can explain its structure and function. Student has reviewed Resolution 1373 and can explain some of its goals and purposes.

- Student has identified some of the banks and other financial institutions that may have useful information about the implementation of Resolution 1373 in their community. Law enforcement has also been identified.

- Student had contributed somewhat to the letter to classmates explaining Resolution 1373 and its connection to terrorism. Student has added to the letter's explanation of the connection between crime and terrorism.

## UNACCEPTABLE

- Student has done some research on the UN Security Council, but cannot fully explain its function and structure. Student can discuss little about Resolution 1373.

- Student has not identified the local resources that implement the Resolution nor has he or she identified local law enforcement. The student's questions for the invited speakers show little understanding of the goals of Resolution 1373.

- Student has not added to the letter to classmates substantively. Student cannot discuss the connection between crime and terrorism.

# Task Sheet

Check off the following tasks as you complete them.

❏ **1.** Research the UN Security Council. Discover what its functions and purposes are and how it is structured. Discuss the significance of having five permanent and ten rotating representatives.

❏ **2.** From the UN web site, access Security Resolution 1373. Read it and make notes on its goals and purposes. Also note how it is implemented and what it calls for UN member nations to do. Discuss the Resolution in a small group.

❏ **3.** Locate members of financial institutions from your area to discuss how the Resolution gets implemented. Locate members of law enforcement agencies who can discuss what they do with information once it is reported to them. In your small group, formulate questions for the speakers designed to clarify how Resolution 1373 is implemented locally.

❏ **4.** After completing your research and talking to the invited speaker, discuss with your small group how Resolution 1373 is related to the regulations imposed on financial institutions and law enforcement. Draw the connections between the goals of Resolution 1373 and the regulations. Describe the connection between crime and terrorism.

❏ **5.** With your group, draft a letter to your fellow classmates explaining what you have learned. Describe the goals of the Resolution, what they require of UN member nations, and the connection between crime and terrorism. Explain how the United States implements the reporting requirements via banks and other financial institutions, and what law-enforcement agencies do with the information once they receive it.

# The First Televised War

## OBJECTIVES

After completing this activity, students will be able to:

- Explain the United States' interest in Vietnam.
- Discuss the reaction in the United States to the Vietnam conflict.
- Describe their community's reaction to key events in the Vietnam conflict.

## OVERVIEW

In this activity, students will explore the foreign policy that led the United States into the Vietnam conflict. Students will research the beginnings of the conflict, trace the U.S. policy that increased U.S. commitment in the region, and describe the public's increased hostility to U.S. involvement. Students will be given specific dates to look up in the archives of local newspapers for information on their community's reaction. Students will be able to identify the supporters and opponents of the Vietnam conflict and determine whether the attitude of the community changed as a result of increased television coverage. Students also will invite veterans of the Vietnam conflict to speak to the class about their experiences. After completing their research, students will create a cartoon expressing their view of the conflict.

## PLANNING

**Suggested Time** Plan to spend at least two 45-minute class periods and two homework assignments on this activity.

**Resources** Students can use any source available, including newspapers, magazines, movies, documentaries, the Internet, or their library to get information.

**Preparation** You may want to have students look at examples of political cartoons to get an idea of how current events are expressed as cartoons. The Veterans of Foreign Wars (VFW) organization may be a source of information about Vietnam veterans who may be willing to talk to the class about their experiences.

## IMPLEMENTATION

1. Discuss the project with the class. You might begin by asking students what they know about the Vietnam conflict and their sources of information. Ask about movies that they may have seen or comments that they may have heard about it. Distribute copies of the Planning Guidelines, Standards for Evaluating Your Work, and Task Sheet to the class. Give students a time frame for completing the project.

2. Have students research U.S. involvement in Vietnam in the library, on the Internet, or in books about the era. Identify important dates, and have students use these dates to research their community's response to these events from materials such as newspaper archives and other historical sources.

3. Have the students contact veterans of the Vietnam conflict. The VFW or other organizations might be helpful in finding local veterans for this purpose. Alternatively, students may visit local VFW headquarters. Have students ask about the experiences veterans had in Vietnam. Explore the treatment they received when they returned home, what it was like to be in the military or to be drafted, whether they were personally for or against the war, and whether their perspective has changed since their return.

4. After students have completed their research and the speakers have addressed the class, have students express their support or opposition to U.S. involvement in Vietnam in political cartoon form.

## ASSESSMENT

To evaluate students' work, use the Standards for Evaluating Work on page 95, along with Rubric 3: Artwork, and Rubric 27: Political Cartoons, in the *Alternative Assessment Handbook* or in a customizable format on the One-Stop Planner.

# Planning Guidelines

In this activity, you will learn about the Vietnam conflict and what events drew the United States into this part of Southeast Asia. You will find out about the political mood in the United States at the time and why the United States eventually felt the need to commit troops to prevent the expansion of communism into the region. You also will hear from veterans of the conflict who were drafted and sent to the area to fight. You can learn from them what it was like to serve in the military during that time. Your research will reveal certain key dates in the history of the conflict. From these dates, you can use local resources to discover exactly how your community reacted in response to events on those dates. You also will learn whether any members of your community participated in any antiwar activities and whether these persons are still active in the community. As a result of what you learn, you will create a political cartoon that depicts how you think you might have felt about the conflict if you had been alive then.

1. Contact the Veterans of Foreign Wars (VFW) or another veterans group in your area and invite veterans of the Vietnam conflict to your class to speak about their experience in Vietnam. Alternatively, you can visit them.

2. Research the events that led the United States into the Vietnam conflict. Find out why the United States felt it necessary to get involved in a region of the world so far away. Discover the key dates in the war and record these dates. You should at least include October 21, 1967 (protest demonstration at the Pentagon); February 24, 1968 (Tet offensive); August 29, 1968 (Chicago Democratic Party Convention confrontation); and May 4, 1970 (Kent State University protest). You might find other dates in the course of your research.

3. After learning about the conflict, develop questions that you would like to ask about the Vietnam experience. Ask the veterans you invite to speak to your class to answer your questions. How was their experience different from or similar to what you expected after doing the research?

4. Use the local library or other sources to research the response of your community to the events that you listed as "key." In your research, what responses did you find from local community leaders? What form did these expressions take? Were there similar activities in your community that mirrored the national responses? Are the people who were involved in these activities still active in your community?

5. When your research is complete and you have spoken with the Vietnam veterans, gauge which side of the conflict you think you would have been on if you had been able to express an opinion at the time. Create a political cartoon that expresses your opinion. Discuss the cartoon with your classmates and compare your feelings with theirs.

# Standards for Evaluating Work

## EXCELLENT

• Student has researched the origins of the conflict and understands the foreign policy that led to U.S. involvement in the region. Student has used many sources of information to gather and complete his or her research. Student has many key dates to offer.

• Student has contacted speakers from local organizations to invite to the class. Student's questions for the speakers are excellent and are designed to shed further light on the events of the day. Student has researched local history and is able to tell how the events affected the local community.

• Student has drawn a political cartoon that is insightful and interesting. It captures the student's feelings about U.S. participation in the Vietnam conflict.

## ACCEPTABLE

• Student has researched the origins of the conflict. Student has some understanding of the foreign policy and key dates but has not used many sources in obtaining data.

• Student has identified the organizations from which speakers can be invited .Student is able to discuss the local reaction to the major events identified. Student's questions for the invited speakers are good.

• Student has drawn a political cartoon. Student's expression of his or her feelings is not clearly reflected in the cartoon.

## UNACCEPTABLE

• Student's research does not adequately show the origins of the conflict, nor does it identify key dates. Student has used only a few resources in the research.

• Student has not identified any organization from which a speaker may be obtained. Student has not thought of cogent questions to ask the invited speakers. Student's local research is not comprehensive and does not describe the local reaction.

• Student's cartoon is off base. Student does not identify a position in the cartoon or has not expressed clearly his or her feelings about the conflict.

## Task Sheet

Check off the following tasks as you complete the activity.

❑ **1.** Obtain the names of speakers who might be available to speak to your class about the Vietnam conflict. Choose these speakers from an organization such as the VFW.

❑ **2.** Research the increased involvement of the United States in Vietnam. Identify key events and write the dates down for further research.

❑ **3.** Identify the community's reaction to these key events in the Vietnam conflict. Use the library or other sources to research how the community reacted.

❑ **4.** When the speakers come to your class, ask them questions about their experiences. How did their experiences match your expectations after the research? How were they treated when they returned home? Have they changed since they returned home?

❑ **5.** After talking to the veterans and researching your community's reaction to the conflict, decide how you think you might have felt during that time. Would you have been a "hawk" or a "dove"? Draw a political cartoon describing your feelings.

# Form 1 United States Census Form

*PLEASE DO NOT FILL OUT THIS FORM.*
*This is not an official census form. It is for informational purposes only.*

**United States**
**Census**
**2000**

U.S. Department of Commerce • Bureau of the Census

This is the official form for all the people at this address. It is quick and easy, and your answers are protected by law. Complete the Census and help your community get what it needs — today and in the future!

## Start Here

Please use a black or blue pen.

**1.** How many people were living or staying in this house, apartment, or mobile home on April 1, 2000?

[    ]   Number of people

**INCLUDE** in this number:
- foster children, roomers, or housemates
- people staying here on April 1, 2000 who have no other permanent place to stay
- people living here most of the time while working, even if they have another place to live

**DO NOT INCLUDE** in this number:
- college students living away while attending college
- people in a correctional facility, nursing home, or mental hospital on April 1, 2000
- Armed Forces personnel living somewhere else
- people who live or stay at another place most of the time

**2.** Is this house, apartment, or mobile home —
*Mark* ⌧

☐ Owned by you or someone in this household with a mortgage or loan?
☐ Owned by you or someone in this household free and clear (without a mortgage or loan)?
☐ Rented for cash rent?
☐ Occupied without payment of cash rent?

**3.** Please answer the following questions for each person living in this house, apartment, or mobile home. Start with the name of one of the people living here who owns, is buying, or rents this house, apartment, or mobile home. If there is no such person, start with any adult living or staying here. We will refer to this person as Person 1.

What is this person's name? *Print name below.*

Last Name
[                    ]

First Name                                    MI
[                    ]

**4.** What is Person 1's telephone number? *We may call this person if we don't understand an answer.*

Area Code + Number
[   ] - [   ] - [   ]

**5.** What is Person 1's sex? *Mark* ⌧
☐ Male        ☐ Female

**6.** What is Person 1's age and what is Person 1's date of birth?
Age on April 1, 2000
[    ]

*Print numbers in boxes.*
Month      Day       Year of birth
[  ]       [  ]      [    ]

→ **NOTE: Please answer BOTH Questions 7 and 8.**

**7.** Is Person 1 Spanish/Hispanic/Latino? *Mark* ⌧

☐ **No,** not Spanish/Hispanic/Latino      ☐ Yes, Puerto Rican
☐ Yes, Mexican, Mexican Am., Chicano      ☐ Yes, Cuban
☐ Yes, other Spanish/Hispanic/Latino — *Print group.* ⬎

[                              ]

**8.** What is Person 1's race? *Mark* ⌧

☐ White
☐ Black, African Am., or Negro
☐ American Indian or Alaska Native — *Print name of enrolled or principal tribe.* ⬎

[                              ]

☐ Asian Indian    ☐ Japanese     ☐ Native Hawaiian
☐ Chinese         ☐ Korean       ☐ Guamanian or Chamorro
☐ Filipino        ☐ Vietnamese   ☐ Samoan
☐ Other Asian — *Print race.* ⬎    ☐ Other Pacific Islander — *Print race.* ⬎

☐ Some other race — *Print race.* ⬎

[                              ]

→ **If more people live here, continue with Person 2.**

OMB No. 0607-0856: Approval Expires 12/31/2000

Form **D-61A**

# Form 1 United States Census Form

## Person 2

Your answers are important!
Every person in the Census counts.

**1. What is Person 2's name?** *Print name below.*
Last Name

First Name      MI

**2. How is this person related to Person 1?** *Mark* [X]

- [ ] Husband/wife
- [ ] Natural-born son/daughter
- [ ] Adopted son/daughter
- [ ] Stepson/stepdaughter
- [ ] Brother/sister
- [ ] Father/mother
- [ ] Grandchild
- [ ] Parent-in-law
- [ ] Son-in-law/daughter-in-law
- [ ] Other relative — *Print exact relationship.* →

If NOT RELATED to Person 1:
- [ ] Roomer, boarder
- [ ] Housemate, roommate
- [ ] Unmarried partner
- [ ] Foster child
- [ ] Other nonrelative *the*

**3. What is this person's sex?** *Mark* [X]
- [ ] Male
- [ ] Female

**4. What is this person's age and what is this person's date of birth?** *Print numbers in boxes.*
Age on April 1, 2000   Month   Day   Year of birth

→ **NOTE: Please answer BOTH Questions 5 and 6.**

**5. Is this person Spanish/Hispanic/Latino?** *Mark* [X]
- [ ] **No,** not Spanish/Hispanic/Latino
- [ ] Yes, Mexican, Mexican Am., Chicano
- [ ] Yes, other Spanish/Hispanic/Latino — *Print group.* ↘
- [ ] Yes, Puerto Rican
- [ ] Yes, Cuban

**6. What is this person's race?** *Mark* [X]
- [ ] White
- [ ] Black, African Am., or Negro
- [ ] American Indian or Alaska Native — *Print name of enrolled or principal tribe.* ↘

- [ ] Asian Indian
- [ ] Chinese
- [ ] Filipino
- [ ] Other Asian — *Print race.* ↘
- [ ] Japanese
- [ ] Korean
- [ ] Vietnamese
- [ ] Native Hawaiian
- [ ] Guamanian or Chamorro
- [ ] Samoan
- [ ] Other Pacific Islander — *Print race.* ↘

- [ ] Some other race — *Print race.* ↘

→ **If more people live here, continue with Person 3.**

## Person 3

Census information helps your community get financial assistance for roads, hospitals, schools, and more.

**1. What is Person 3's name?** *Print name below.*
Last Name

First Name      MI

**2. How is this person related to Person 1?** *Mark* [X]

- [ ] Husband/wife
- [ ] Natural-born son/daughter
- [ ] Adopted son/daughter
- [ ] Stepson/stepdaughter
- [ ] Brother/sister
- [ ] Father/mother
- [ ] Grandchild
- [ ] Parent-in-law
- [ ] Son-in-law/daughter-in-law
- [ ] Other relative — *Print exact relationship.* →

If NOT RELATED to Person 1:
- [ ] Roomer, boarder
- [ ] Housemate, roommate
- [ ] Unmarried partner
- [ ] Foster child
- [ ] Other nonrelative *the*

**3. What is this person's sex?** *Mark* [X]
- [ ] Male
- [ ] Female

**4. What is this person's age and what is this person's date of birth?** *Print numbers in boxes.*
Age on April 1, 2000   Month   Day   Year of birth

→ **NOTE: Please answer BOTH Questions 5 and 6.**

**5. Is this person Spanish/Hispanic/Latino?** *Mark* [X]
- [ ] **No,** not Spanish/Hispanic/Latino
- [ ] Yes, Mexican, Mexican Am., Chicano
- [ ] Yes, other Spanish/Hispanic/Latino — *Print group.* ↘
- [ ] Yes, Puerto Rican
- [ ] Yes, Cuban

**6. What is this person's race?** *Mark* [X]
- [ ] White
- [ ] Black, African Am., or Negro
- [ ] American Indian or Alaska Native — *Print name of enrolled or principal tribe.* ↘

- [ ] Asian Indian
- [ ] Chinese
- [ ] Filipino
- [ ] Other Asian — *Print race.* ↘
- [ ] Japanese
- [ ] Korean
- [ ] Vietnamese
- [ ] Native Hawaiian
- [ ] Guamanian or Chamorro
- [ ] Samoan
- [ ] Other Pacific Islander — *Print race.* ↘

- [ ] Some other race — *Print race.* ↘

→ **If more people live here, continue with Person 4.**

# Form 2 Voter Registration Form

## Voter Registration Form

**You can use this form to:**
- register to vote.
- update your current registration if you have changed your address or name.

*Instructions:* **Please type or print clearly** with a black pen.

1. Your last name, full legal first name, middle name or initial and any suffix such as Jr., Sr., etc.

2-4. House number, street, city and zip code for your current residence.

5-6. Mailing address *only* if it is different from your residence address, including post office box if applicable. County of residence.

7. The 2-digit number of the month, the day and the year you were born — example: 04-24-45.

8. The city and state where you were born. If born outside the U.S., indicate city and/or country.

9-10. Social Security number and phone number are voluntary.

11. Previous address. *Complete this section only if you are, or have been, registered to vote.*

12. Complete only if you have changed your name since last registration. Put your former legal name in the first box; your former legal signature in the second box.

13. Signature. Your complete legal signature or mark *should not touch surrounding lines or type.* If signature is a mark, include name and address of the person who witnessed the mark. Date — 2-digit month, day and year.

---

**To qualify to vote, you must be:**

(1) a U.S. citizen;
(2) 18 years old on or before the general election day;
(3) a resident of Ohio for at least 30 days;
(4) registered to vote at least 30 days before election day.

**Notice:** Your registration or change must be **received or postmarked** 30 days before an election at which you intend to vote. You will be notified by your county board of elections of the location where you vote.

Do you want to register to vote or update your current voter registration? ❏ Yes ❏ No If you do not check a box, we will assume you choose not to register to vote.

---

FOLD HERE

---

**Are you a U.S. citizen?** ❏ Yes ❏ No **If you answered NO, do not complete this form.**

**This is an application for a** ❏ New Registration ❏ Address Change ❏ Name Change

| 1. Last Name | First Name | Middle Name or Initial | Jr., II, etc. |
|---|---|---|---|

| 2. House Number and Street (Enter new address if changed) | Apt. or Lot # | 3. City or Post Office | 4. Zip Code |
|---|---|---|---|

| 5. Additional Rural or Mailing Address (if necessary) | 6. County where you live |
|---|---|

FOR BOARD USE ONLY
SEC4010 (Rev. 1/99)

| 7. Birthdate (MO - DAY - YR) | 8. Birthplace (City and State) | 9. Social Security No. (voluntary) | 10. Phone No. (voluntary) |
|---|---|---|---|

City, Village, Twp.

**11. ADDRESS CHANGE ONLY - PREVIOUS ADDRESS**

Previous House Number and Street

Ward

| Previous City or Post Office | County | State |
|---|---|---|

Precinct

| 12. CHANGE OF NAME ONLY | Former Legal Name | Former Signature |
|---|---|---|

School Dist.

I declare under penalty of election falsification I am a citizen of the United States, will have lived in this state for 30 days immediately preceding the next election, and I will be at least 18 years of age at the time of the general election.

Cong. Dist.

**13. Signature of Applicant →**

Senate Dist.

Date_____/_____/_____
    MO   DAY   YR

House Dist.

Information that will remain confidential and will be used only for voter registration purposes: 1) the office where you submit your voter registration application or 2) the fact that you have declined to register. **WHOEVER COMMITS ELECTION FALSIFICATION IS GUILTY OF A FELONY OF THE FIFTH DEGREE.**

---

# Form 3 Optional Application for Federal Employment

**OPTIONAL APPLICATION FOR FEDERAL EMPLOYMENT – OF 612**

Form Approved
OMB No. 3206-0219

## Section A – Applicant Information

★ Use Standard State Postal Codes (abbreviations). If outside the United States of America, and you do not have a military address, type or print "OV" in the State field (Block 6c) and fill in the Country field (Block 6e) below, leaving the Zip Code field (Block 6d) blank.

| 1. Job title in announcement | 2. Grade(s) applying for | 3. Announcement number |
|---|---|---|
| 4a. Last name | 4b. First and middle names | 5. Social Security Number |

| 6a. Mailing address ★ | 7. Phone numbers (include area code if within the United States of America) 7a. Daytime |
|---|---|

| 6b. City | 6c. State | 6d. Zip Code | 7b. Evening |
|---|---|---|---|

6e. Country (if not within the United States of America)

8. Email address (if available)

## Section B – Work Experience

Describe your paid and nonpaid work experience related to this job for which you are applying. Do not attach job description.

1. Job title (if Federal, include series and grade)

| 2. From (mm/yyyy) | 3. To (mm/yyyy) | 4. Salary per $ | 5. Hours per week |
|---|---|---|---|

| 6. Employer's name and address | 7. Supervisor's name and phone number 7a. Name 7b. Phone |
|---|---|

8. May we contact your current supervisor?   Yes ☐   No ☐
If we need to contact your current supervisor before making an offer, we will contact you first.

9. Describe your duties and accomplishments

## Section C – Additional Work Experience

1. Job title (if Federal, include series and grade)

| 2. From (mm/yyyy) | 3. To (mm/yyyy) | 4. Salary per $ | 5. Hours per week |
|---|---|---|---|

| 6. Employer's name and address | 7. Supervisor's name and phone number 7a. Name 7b. Phone |
|---|---|

8. Describe your duties and accomplishments

U.S. Office of Personnel Management
Previous edition usable

NSN 7540-01-351-9178
50612-101

Page 1 of 2

Optional Form 612
Revised December 2002

Copyright © by Holt, Rinehart and Winston. All rights reserved.

Holt Civics     (100)     Community Service & Participation Handbook

# Form 3 Optional Application for Federal Employment

| Section D – Education | | | | | | |
|---|---|---|---|---|---|---|
| 1. Last High School (HS)/GED school. Give the school's name, city, state, ZIP Code (if known), and year diploma or GED received: | | | | | | |

2. Mark highest level completed:    Some HS ☐    HS/GED ☐    Associate ☐    Bachelor ☐    Master ☐    Doctoral ☐

| 3. Colleges and universities attended. Do not attach a copy of your transcript unless requested. | | | Total Credits Earned | | Major(s) | Degree (if any), Year Received |
|---|---|---|---|---|---|---|
| | | | Semester | Quarter | | |
| 3a. Name | | | | | | |
| City | State | Zip Code | | | | |
| 3b. Name | | | | | | |
| City | State | Zip Code | | | | |
| 3c. Name | | | | | | |
| City | State | Zip Code | | | | |

## Section E – Other Qualifications

Job-related training courses (give title and year). Job-related skills (other languages, computer software/hardware, tools, machinery, typing speed, etc.). Job-related certificates and licenses (current only). Job-related honors, awards, and special accomplishments (publications, memberships in professional/honor societies, leadership activities, public speaking, and performance awards). Give dates, but do **not** send documents unless requested.

## Section F – General

1a. Are you a U.S. citizen?    Yes ☐    No ☐    →    1b. If no, give the Country of your citizenship

2a. Do you claim veterans' preference?    No ☐    Yes ☐    →    If yes, mark your claim of 5 or 10 points below.

2b.    5 points ☐    →    Attach your *Report of Separation from Active Duty* (DD 214) or other proof.

2c.    10 points ☐    →    Attach an *Application for 10-Point Veterans' Preference* (SF 15) and proof required.

| 3. Were you ever a Federal civilian employee?    No ☐    Yes ☐    →    If yes, list highest civilian grade for the following: | | | |
|---|---|---|---|
| 3a. Series | 3b. Grade | 3c. From *(mm/yyyy)* | 3d. To *(mm/yyyy)* |

4. Are you eligible for reinstatement based on career or career-conditional Federal status?    No ☐    Yes ☐
   If requested in the vacancy announcement, attach *Notification of Personnel Action* (SF 50), as proof.

## Section G – Applicant Certification

I certify that, to the best of my knowledge and belief, all of the information on and attached to this application is true, correct, complete, and made in good faith. I understand that false or fraudulent information on or attached to this application may be grounds for not hiring me or for firing me after I begin work, and may be punishable by fine or imprisonment. I understand that any information I give may be investigated.

| 1a. Signature | 1b. Date *(mm/dd/yyyy)* |
|---|---|

U.S. Office of Personnel Management     NSN 7540-01-351-9178     Page 2 of 2     Optional Form 612
Previous edition usable     50612-101     Revised December 2002

# Form 4 U.S. Government Printing Office Order Form

 United States Government
**INFORMATION**
PUBLICATIONS ★ PERIODICALS ★ ELECTRONIC PRODUCTS

ORDER BY MAIL    Superintendent of Documents
PO Box 371954
Pittsburgh, PA 15250–7954

Order Processing Code

**✳ 3264**

 ORDER BY PHONE:
(202) 512-1800
7:30 a.m. - 4:30 p.m.
eastern time

 ORDER BY FAX:
(202) 512-2250
24 hours a day

 ORDER ONLINE:
• orders@gpo.gov
• www.access.gpo.gov/su_docs/
  sale/prf/prf.html
  24 hours a day

Please type or print

Publications

| Qty. | Stock Number | Title | Price | Total Price |
|------|--------------|-------|-------|-------------|
|      |              |       |       |             |
|      |              |       |       |             |
|      |              |       |       |             |
|      |              |       |       |             |
|      |              |       |       |             |
|      |              |       |       |             |
|      |              |       |       |             |
|      |              |       |       |             |
|      |              |       |       |             |
|      |              |       |       |             |
|      |              |       | Total for Publications | |

Subscriptions

| Qty. | List ID | Title | Price | Total Price |
|------|---------|-------|-------|-------------|
|      |         |       |       |             |
|      |         |       |       |             |
|      |         |       |       |             |
|      |         |       |       |             |
|      |         |       |       |             |
|      |         |       |       |             |
|      |         |       | Total for Subscriptions | |
|      |         |       | Total Cost of Order | |

NOTE: Prices include regular domestic postage and handling and are subject to change. International customers please add 25%.

Check method of payment:
❏ Check payable to Superintendent of Documents
❏ GPO Deposit Account ⬚⬚⬚⬚⬚⬚⬚—⬚
❏ VISA  ❏ MasterCard  ❏ Discover/Novus

⬚⬚⬚⬚ (expiration date)

Personal name        (Please type or print)

Company name

Street address

Authorizing signature        12/98

City, State, Zip code

Daytime phone including area code

If you have questions regarding my order
Call ( ) _____ daytime
Fax ( ) _____
or Email _____

Please return order form with payment.

Thank you for your interest in U.S. Government Information. ALL SALES ARE FINAL.

# Form 5 Driver's License/Identification Application

## WYOMING DRIVER LICENSE/IDENTIFICATION CARD APPLICATION
### To be completed by all applicants in black ink

**Please Print:**

Legal Name: (Last)_____ , (First)_____ (Middle)_____

Mailing Address:_____
Box Number/Street       City       State       Zip Code

Residential Address:_____
Number & Street       City       State       Zip Code

Date of Birth: _____/_____/_____    Phone: (   )_____
Month   Day   Year

Social Security Number: _____ Do you want your SSN to show on your license/ID? ☐ **YES** ☐ **NO**

1. Are you a United States Citizen?   ☐ **YES** ☐ **NO**   Place of Birth_____
City       State or Country

2. Are you a Wyoming Resident?   ☐ **YES** ☐ **NO**   If no, are you: ☐ **Active-Duty Military** ☐ **Fulltime WY College Student**

3. Has your current driver license or identification card been:   ☐ **lost?** ☐ **stolen?** ☐ **taken by law enforcement?** ☐ **n/a**

4. Is your privilege to drive currently suspended, cancelled, revoked or denied in this or any other state?   ☐ **YES** ☐ **NO**

5. Do you wish to be an **organ donor**?   ☐ **YES** ☐ **NO**    (If under 18 yrs., must have parent's permission to be a donor)

*The above-named minor has my permission to be an organ donor.* ☐ YES ☐ NO _____Parent/Guardian

Signature

## MEDICAL HISTORY

6. Do you have **paralysis** and/or **missing limbs**?   ☐ **YES** ☐ **NO**

     If yes, please describe:_____

7. Have you **lost consciousness**, due to a **seizure**, **stroke**, or **insulin shock**, within the previous five (5) year period?

     ☐ **YES** ☐ **NO**    If yes, what caused the loss of consciousness?_____

List any **physical** or **mental** conditions you are currently being treated for:_____

## APPLICANTS FOR COMMERCIAL CLASS LICENSES & NON-COMMERCIAL CLASS (A) & (B) ONLY

8. Are you applying for a Commercial Driver License (CDL) and subject to Part 391 of the Federal Motor Carrier Safety

     Regulations?   ☐ **YES** ☐ **NO**   If exempt, what is your occupation?_____

9. Do you possess a valid Federal DOT Medical card?   ☐ **YES** ☐ **NO**   Expiration Date:_____

10. Are you being treated for:   ☐ **Epilepsy**? ☐ **Heart Disease**? ☐ **Insulin Dependent Diabetes**? ☐ **High Blood Pressure**?

11. Do you consent to the release of your personal information by the Wyoming Department of Transportation for bulk distribution
surveys, marketing or solicitations?   ☐ **YES** ☐ **NO**

NOTE: Personal Information means information that identifies a person, including an individualís photograph or computerized image, signature, social security number, driver identification number, name, address, telephone number, and medical or disability information.

I hereby authorize the release of my driving record to authorized recipients. I hereby certify under penalties of law, that the above information is true and correct. Use of a false or fictitious name or knowingly making a false statement or concealing a material fact in this application may result in a fine or imprisonment or both, and the cancellation of your Wyoming driver license/identification card.

_____   _____   Minor's Release: I hereby certify under penalties of law, that I   _____
Applicant's Signature       Date       am the legal parent/guardian having custody of the minor and   Date
                        hereby verify that the above information is true and correct.

## VISION SCREENING   (to be completed by Driver License Examiner or a Vision Specialist)

Right      Left      Both

Visual Acuity: 20/_____ 20/_____ 20/_____    Corrective Lenses/Contacts? ☐ **YES** ☐ **NO**

Depth Perception? ☐ **YES** ☐ **NO**    Horizontal Field of Vision:   **Right Eye:** _____degrees   **Left Eye:** _____degrees

_____     _____
Signature of Vision Specialist/Examiner     Date of Exam

COMMENTS/RESTRICTIONS:_____

**\*\*EXAMINER'S USE ONLY\*\***                        MVID # _____

Verification Document, Number & State: _____

Applicantís Driver License or Identification Number: _____ State/Issue Date: _____

Surrendered driver license/ID for invalidation? ☐ YES ☐ NO   Class/Endorsmnt applied for:_____ Service:_____

Clearance Verification:   **CDLIS** ☐   **PDPS** ☐ ELG/LIC ☐ NOT   **RIS** ☐ Clear ☐ Not Clear   ☐ Attachment_____

Change of Name, DOB & SSN from previous: ☐ YES ☐ NO   If yes, what changed?_____

TESTING:   Written:   ☐ Rules of the Road ☐ Motorcycle ☐ Signs/Ctrls   Form:_____ Score:_____

           Skills:   ☐ Regular Skills   ☐ AltMOST   ☐ Re-Exam   ☐ CDL   Score:_____

COMMENTS:_____

_____     _____
Examiner's Signature     Date

# Form 6 Application for License Plates or Parking Permits for Persons with Severe Disabilities

MV-664.1 (2/04)      New York State Department of Motor Vehicles
**APPLICATION FOR A PARKING PERMIT OR LICENSE PLATES,**
**FOR PERSONS WITH SEVERE DISABILITIES**

Take this completed application to the **issuing agent in the area where you live**. Also, if you have a **NYS driver license or an ID card issued by NYS DMV**, bring it with you when you apply for the permit.

## Part 1 INFORMATION ABOUT PERSON WITH DISABILITY —*(Please print, and sign by the arrow.)*

| Last Name | First | M.I. | Telephone No. ( ) |
|---|---|---|---|

| Address: No. and Street | Apt. No. | City | State | Zip Code |
|---|---|---|---|---|

| Date of Birth | ☐ Male ☐ Female | I am applying for ☐ License Plates *(Apply to DMV.)* ☐ Parking Permit *(Apply to local issuing agent.)* |
|---|---|---|

Do you have license plates for persons with disabilities?   ☐ Yes - My license plate number is:_____   ☐ No

**See Note on Page 2**

▶ _____    _____
**(Signature of Person with Disability or Signature of Parent or Guardian)** — *If signed by a parent or*   (Date)
*guardian, please state your relationship to the person with the disability after your signature.*

## Part 2 MEDICAL CERTIFICATION—*This section must be completed only by a Medical Doctor (MD), Doctor of Osteopathy (DO) or Doctor of Podiatric Medicine (DPM). Please certify whether the patient's disability is permanent or temporary.*

**Check the box(es) that describe the disability, and fill in the diagnosis:**

☐ **TEMPORARY DISABILITY:** A person with a temporary disability is any person who is temporarily **unable to ambulate without the aid of an assisting device**, such as a brace, cane, crutch, prosthetic device, another person, wheelchair, walker or other assistive device. (Temporary permits are issued for periods of six months or less.)   **Expected Recovery Date** _____

**Diagnosis:**_____

**What assistive device is needed?** _____

☐ **PERMANENT DISABILITY:** A "severely disabled" person is any person with one or more of the PERMANENT impairments, disabilities or conditions listed below, which limit mobility.
**Diagnosis:**_____   Please **check the conditions that apply:**

☐ Uses portable oxygen   ☐ Legally blind   ☐ Limited or no use of one or both legs   ☐ Unable to walk 200 ft. without stopping

☐ Neuromuscular dysfunction that severely limits mobility   ☐ Class III or IV cardiac condition. (American Heart Assoc. standards)

☐ Severely limited in ability to walk due to an arthritic, neurological or orthopedic condition

☐ Restricted by lung disease to such an extent that forced (respiratory) expiratory volume for one second, when measured by spirometry, is less than one liter, or the arterial oxygen tension is less than sixty mm/hg of room air at rest

☐ Has a physical or mental impairment or condition not listed above which constitutes an equal degree of disability, and which imposes <u>unusual hardship in the <u>use of public transportation</u> and <u>prevents</u> the person from <u>getting around without great difficulty</u>. **EXPLAIN HOW THIS DISABILITY LIMITS FUNCTIONAL MOBILITY.**

| MD/DO/DPM Name | Professional License No. |
|---|---|

| MD/DO/DPM Address | Telephone No. ( ) |
|---|---|

**See Note on Page 2**

▶ _____    _____
(MD/DO/DPM Signature)   (Date)

## Part 3 FILE INFORMATION *(For Issuing Agent Use Only)*

☐ Blue ☐ Red  **Parking Permit No.** _____   Date Issued:_____   Date Expires: _____

☐ First ☐ Second   9-digit number from NYS Driver License/ID Card _____

☐ Denied ☐ Revoked   Reason:_____
                                                                                        (Date)
▶ _____    _____
(Issuing Agent)   (Locality)

PAGE 1 OF 2

# Form 7 Application for Certificate of Title

## 1 — OWNER / APPLICANT INFORMATION

| Customer Number | Unit Number | Fleet Number |
|---|---|---|

☐ OR  ☐ AND  NOTE: When joint ownership, please indicate if "or" or "and" is to be shown on title when issued. **If neither box is checked, the title will be issued with "and".**

| Owner's First Name, Full Middle/Maiden Name, Last Name | Date of Birth | Sex | FL Driver License or FEID Number |
|---|---|---|---|
| Co-Owner's First Name, Full Middle/Maiden Name, Last Name | Date of Birth | Sex | FL Driver License or FEID Number |
| Lessee's First Name, Full Middle/Maiden Name, Last Name | Date of Birth | Sex | FL Driver License or FEID Number |

| Owner's Mailing Address (Mandatory) | City | State | Zip |
|---|---|---|---|
| Co-Owner's or Lessee's Mailing Address (Mandatory) | City | State | Zip |
| Owner's or Lessee's Street Address in Florida (Mandatory) | City | State | Zip |

| Mail to Customer Name (If Different From Above Owner) | Date of Birth | Sex | FL Driver License or FEID Number |
|---|---|---|---|
| Mail to Customer Address (If Different From Above Mailing Address) | City | State | Zip |

## 2 — MOTOR VEHICLE, MOBILE HOME OR VESSEL DESCRIPTION

| Vehicle/Vessel Identification Number | Make/Manufacturer | Year | Body | Color | Florida Title Number |
|---|---|---|---|---|---|
| Previous State of Issue | License Plate or Vessel Registration Number | Weight | Length Ft  in. | BHP/CC | GVW/LOC | Florida Current Date of Issue |

**TYPE**
☐ Open Motorboat ☐ Houseboat ☐ Personal Watercraft
☐ Cabin Motorboat ☐ Pontoon ☐ Canoe
☐ Auxiliary Sailboat ☐ Airboat ☐ Other _____ Specify
☐ Inflatable ☐ Sailboat

**HULL MATERIAL**
☐ Wood ☐ Aluminum
☐ Fiberglass ☐ Steel
☐ Wood/Fiberglass
☐ Other _____ Specify

**PROPULSION**
☐ Outboard ☐ Sail
☐ Inboard ☐ Air Propelled
☐ Inboard/Outboard
☐ Other _____ Specify

**FUEL**
☐ Gas
☐ Diesel
☐ Electric
☐ Other _____ Specify

***DRAFT OF VESSEL**
(The depth of water a vessel draws)
FT. _____ IN. _____
*For all vessels 26' or more in length and all sailboats

**USE OF VESSEL**
☐ Recreational (Pleasure) ☐ Commercial Blue Crab ☐ Commercial Stone Crab
☐ Dealer/Manuf. ☐ Commercial Fish ☐ Commercial Live Bait ☐ Commercial Shrimp Recip.
☐ Exempt ☐ Hire (Livery) ☐ Commercial Mackerel ☐ Commercial Shrimp Non-Recip.
☐ Government ☐ Commercial Sponge ☐ Commercial Oyster ☐ Commercial Spiney Lobster
☐ Commercial Charter ☐ Commercial Other

| | Owner | Co-Owner | PREVIOUS OUT-OF-STATE REGISTRATION NUMBER: |
|---|---|---|---|
| Are you a Florida resident? | ☐ Yes ☐ No | ☐ Yes ☐ No | |
| Are you an alien? | ☐ Yes ☐ No | ☐ Yes ☐ No | |

Previously Federally Documented Vessel, Attach Copy of:       State of Principal Use
☐ U.S. Coast Guard Release From Documentation Form; or  ☐ Copy of Canceled Documentation Papers

## 3 — BRANDS AND USAGE (Check Applicable Boxes)

☐ Vehicle is: ☐ Vessel is: ☐ SHORT TERM LEASED ☐ LONG TERM LEASED ☐ REBUILT ☐ POLICE VEHICLE ☐ PRIVATE USE ☐ TAXI CAB ☐ FLOOD VEHICLE
☐ ASSEMBLED FROM PARTS ☐ MANUFACTURER'S BUY BACK ☐ REPLICA ☐ COMBINED ☐ KIT CAR ☐ GLIDER KIT

## 4 — LIENHOLDER INFORMATION

| Check if ELT Customer ☐ | Customer # or FEID # or DL# and Sex and Date of Birth | Date of Lien | Lienholder Name |
|---|---|---|---|
| Lienholder Address | City | | State | Zip |

☐ If Lienholder authorizes the Department to send the motor vehicle or mobile home title to the owner, check box and countersign: _____
(Does not apply to Vessels) If box above is not checked, title will be mailed to the first lienholder.    (Signature of Lienholder's Representative)

## 5 — TRANSFER TYPE

IF OWNERSHIP HAS TRANSFERRED, HOW WAS VEHICLE, MOBILE HOME, VESSEL ACQUIRED? ☐ SALE ☐ GIFT ☐ REPOSSESSION ☐ COURT ORDER
☐ OTHER SPECIFY _____ DATE ACQUIRED _____ ☐ NEW _____ ☐ USED _____

## 6 — ODOMETER DECLARATION

WARNING: Federal and State law requires that you state the mileage in connection with an application for a Certificate of Title. Failure to complete or providing a false statement may result in fines or imprisonment

I STATE THAT THIS MOTOR VEHICLE'S ☐ 5 DIGIT OR ☐ 6 DIGIT ODOMETER NOW READS ☐☐☐,☐☐☐ ☐☐ (no tenths) MILES, DATE READ ___ / ___ / ___ AND TO THE BEST OF MY KNOWLEDGE THAT IT REFLECTS THE **ACTUAL MILEAGE** OF THE VEHICLE DESCRIBED IN THIS DOCUMENT **UNLESS ONE OF THE FOLLOWING IS CHECKED:**

**CAUTION:**
DO NOT CHECK ☐ 1. I HEREBY CERTIFY THAT, TO THE BEST OF MY KNOWLEDGE, THE ODOMETER READING REFLECTS THE AMOUNT OF MILEAGE **IN EXCESS OF ITS MECHANICAL LIMITS.**
IF ACTUAL MILEAGE ☐ 2. I HEREBY CERTIFY THAT THE ODOMETER READING **IS NOT THE ACTUAL MILEAGE.** **WARNING - ODOMETER DISCREPANCY**

## 7 — DEALER SALES TAX REPORT

| FLORIDA SALES TAX REGISTRATION NUMBER | DATE OF SALE | DEALER LICENSE NUMBER | AMOUNT OF TAX | DEALER / AGENT SIGNATURE |
|---|---|---|---|---|

HSMV 82040 (Rev. 03/02) S          http://www.hsmv.state.fl.us

# Form 7 Application for Certificate of Title

## 8 — MOTOR VEHICLE IDENTIFICATION NUMBER VERIFICATION

THIS SECTION REQUIRES A PHYSICAL INSPECTION AND A VERIFICATION OF THE VEHICLE IDENTIFICATION NUMBER (VIN) OF THE MOTOR VEHICLE DESCRIBED ON THIS FORM BY A LICENSED DEALER, FLORIDA NOTARY PUBLIC, POLICE OFFICER, OR FLORIDA DIVISION OF MOTOR VEHICLES EMPLOYEE OR TAX COLLECTOR EMPLOYEE. **IF THE VIN IS VERIFIED BY AN OUT OF STATE MOTOR VEHICLE DEALER, THE VERIFICATION MUST BE SUBMITTED ON THEIR LETTERHEAD STATIONERY.** COMPLETE THIS SECTION ON ALL USED MOTOR VEHICLES, INCLUDING TRAILERS, (WITH ABBREVIATION OF "TL" WITH A WEIGHT OF 2,000 POUNDS OR MORE) NOT CURRENTLY TITLED IN FLORIDA.

I, the undersigned, certify that I have physically inspected the above described vehicle and find the vehicle identification number to be: _____

(Vehicle Identification Number)

| DATE | SIGNATURE | PRINTED NAME |
|---|---|---|

Law Enforcement Officer Or Florida Dealer's Name _____     Badge# or Florida Dealer # _____

DMV/Tax Collector Employee _____     Florida Compliance Examiner/Inspector Badge or ID Number _____     Notary Stamp or Seal

COMMISSIONED NAME OF FLORIDA NOTARY: _____     NOTARY'S SIGNATURE _____

(Print, type or Stamp)

## 9 — SALES TAX EXEMPTION CERTIFICATION

THE PURCHASE OF A RECREATIONAL VEHICLE TO BE OFFERED FOR RENT AS LIVING ACCOMMODATIONS DOES NOT QUALIFY FOR EXEMPTION. I CERTIFY THE RECREATIONAL VEHICLE, MOBILE HOME OR VESSEL DESCRIBED HAS BEEN PURCHASED AND IS EXEMPT FROM THE SALES TAX IMPOSED BY CHAPTER 212, FLORIDA STATUTES, BY:

_____

CONSUMER'S CERTIFICATE OF EXEMPTION NUMBER

❏ PURCHASER (STATE AGENCIES, COUNTIES, ETC.) HOLDS VALID EXEMPTION CERTIFICATE

❏ MOTOR VEHICLE    ❏ MOBILE HOME    ❏ VESSEL WILL BE USED EXCLUSIVELY FOR RENTAL _____

SALES TAX REGISTRATION NUMBER

I hereby certify that ownership of the motor vehicle, mobile home or vessel described on this application, is not subject to Florida Sales and Use Tax for the following reason:    ❏ INHERITANCE    ❏ GIFT

❏ DIVORCE DECREE    ❏ TRANSFER BETWEEN HUSBAND AND WIFE    ❏ EVEN TRADE OR TRADE DOWN    (State the facts of the even trade or trade down and the transferor information, including the transferor's name and address, below under "Other: Explain.")

❏ OTHER: (EXPLAIN) _____
_____

**NOTE:** ANY PRESUMPTION, REGARDING THE TAXABILITY OF AIRCRAFT, BOATS, MOBILE HOMES, MOTOR VEHICLES, OR OTHER VEHICLES OF A CLASS OR TYPE REQUIRED TO BE REGISTERED, LICENSED, TITLED OR DOCUMENTED IN THIS STATE OR BY THE UNITED STATES GOVERNMENT, ESTABLISHED BY RULE 12A-1.007, F.A.C., MAY BE REBUTTED ONLY BY CLEAR AND CONVINCING EVIDENCE TO THE CONTRARY. DECLARATIONS AFTER-THE-FACT ARE OF LITTLE VALUE AS EVIDENCE BECAUSE OF THEIR SELF-SERVING NATURE AND WILL BE GIVEN LITTLE WEIGHT.

## 10 — REPOSSESSION DECLARATION

IF CHECKED, THE FOLLOWING CERTIFICATIONS ARE MADE BY THE APPLICANT:

❏ I CERTIFY THAT: (1) THIS MOTOR VEHICLE, MOBILE HOME OR VESSEL WAS REPOSSESSED UPON DEFAULT IN THE TERMS OF THE LIEN INSTRUMENT, (2) FOR MOTOR VEHICLES OR MOBILE HOMES, A CERTIFIED COPY OF WHICH IS ATTACHED TO THIS APPLICATION (3) FOR VESSELS, A PHOTOCOPY OF WHICH IS ATTACHED TO THIS APPLICATION AND (4) THE MOTOR VEHICLE, MOBILE HOME OR VESSEL IS NOW IN MY POSSESSION.

❏ I CERTIFY THAT THE SALES CONTRACT FOR THE IDENTIFIED MOTOR VEHICLE, MOBILE HOME OR VESSEL WAS PURCHASED ON (DATE) _____ FROM _____

## 11 — NON-USE AND OTHER CERTIFICATIONS

IF CHECKED, THE FOLLOWING CERTIFICATIONS ARE MADE BY THE APPLICANT:

❏ THE VEHICLE IDENTIFIED WILL NOT BE OPERATED ON THE STREETS AND HIGHWAYS OF THIS STATE.

❏ I CERTIFY THAT THE CERTIFICATE OF TITLE IS LOST OR DESTROYED.    ❏ THE VESSEL IDENTIFIED WILL NOT BE OPERATED ON THE WATERS OF THIS STATE.

❏ OTHER: (EXPLAIN) _____

## 12 — APPLICATION ATTESTMENT AND SIGNATURES

I/WE PHYSICALLY INSPECTED THE ODOMETER AND I/WE FURTHER AGREE TO DEFEND THE TITLE AGAINST ALL CLAIMS.

**UNDER PENALTIES OF PERJURY, I DECLARE THAT I HAVE READ THE FOREGOING DOCUMENT AND THAT THE FACTS STATED IN IT ARE TRUE.**

_____ Date _____     _____ Date _____

SIGNATURE OF APPLICANT (OWNER)     SIGNATURE OF APPLICANT (CO-OWNER)

## 13 — RELEASE OF SPOUSE OR HEIRS INTEREST

The undersigned person(s), state as follows: That _____ of _____ County, Florida died on the _____ day of _____ , 20 _____    ❏ testate (with a will)    ❏ intestate (without a will)  and left surviving (him/her) the following beneficiaries:

Signature(s) of surviving spouse, co-owner and/or heirs. More than one form HSMV 82040 may be used for additional signatures.

UNDER PENALTIES OF PERJURY, I DECLARE THAT I HAVE READ THE FOREGOING DOCUMENT AND THAT THE FACTS STATED IN IT ARE TRUE.

| Print or Type Name of Spouse, Co-owner or Heir(s) | Signature of Spouse, Co-Owner or Heir(s) |
|---|---|

That at the time of death the decedent was owner of the motor vehicle, mobile home or vessel described in section 2 of this form. That the estate is not indebted, and the assets of the estate, excluding this motor vehicle, mobile home or vessel are sufficient to pay all just claims and that no probate proceedings have been instituted upon the estate. That the person(s) signing above hereby releases all their right, title, interest and claim as heirs at law, legatees, devisee, or otherwise to the aforesaid motor vehicle, mobile home or vessel to:

_____

Name of Applicant (Print or Type)

RESIDENTS OF FLORIDA AND ALL VESSEL OWNERS, RESIDING IN FLORIDA OR OUT OF STATE, SHOULD SUBMIT THIS FORM AND ALL REQUIRED DOCUMENTATION TO A LOCAL FLORIDA TAX COLLECTOR'S OFFICE OR THE FLORIDA TAX COLLECTOR'S OFFICE LOCATED IN THE APPLICANT'S COUNTY OF RESIDENCE FOR PROCESSING.

HSMV 82040 (Rev 03/02) S     http://www.hsmv.state.fl.us

# Form 8 Form 1040

**Form 1040**
Department of the Treasury—Internal Revenue Service
**U.S. Individual Income Tax Return** **2005** (99) IRS Use Only—Do not write or staple in this space.

For the year Jan. 1–Dec. 31, 2005, or other tax year beginning _____ , 2005, ending _____ , 20 ____ | OMB No. 1545-0074

**Label**
(See instructions on page 16.)
**Use the IRS label.**
Otherwise, please print or type.

**L A B E L    H E R E**

| Your first name and initial | Last name | | Your social security number |
| If a joint return, spouse's first name and initial | Last name | | Spouse's social security number |
| Home address (number and street). If you have a P.O. box, see page 16. | Apt. no. | ▲ You **must** enter your SSN(s) above. ▲ |
| City, town or post office, state, and ZIP code. If you have a foreign address, see page 16. | | Checking a box below will not change your tax or refund. |

**Presidential Election Campaign** ▶ Check here if you, or your spouse if filing jointly, want $3 to go to this fund (see page 16) ▶ ☐ **You** ☐ **Spouse**

**Filing Status**
Check only one box.

1 ☐ Single
2 ☐ Married filing jointly (even if only one had income)
3 ☐ Married filing separately. Enter spouse's SSN above and full name here. ▶
4 ☐ Head of household (with qualifying person). (See page 17.) If the qualifying person is a child but not your dependent, enter this child's name here. ▶
5 ☐ Qualifying widow(er) with dependent child (see page 17)

**Exemptions**

6a ☐ **Yourself.** If someone can claim you as a dependent, **do not** check box 6a . . . .
b ☐ **Spouse** . . . . . . . . . . . . . . . . . . . . . . . .

| Boxes checked on 6a and 6b ____ |
| No. of children on 6c who: |
| • lived with you ____ |
| • did not live with you due to divorce or separation (see page 20) ____ |
| Dependents on 6c not entered above ____ |
| Add numbers on lines above ▶ ☐ |

c **Dependents:**

| (1) First name    Last name | (2) Dependent's social security number | (3) Dependent's relationship to you | (4) ✔ if qualifying child for child tax credit (see page 19) |
| --- | --- | --- | --- |
| | | | ☐ |
| | | | ☐ |
| | | | ☐ |
| | | | ☐ |

If more than four dependents, see page 19.

d Total number of exemptions claimed . . . . . . . . . . . . . . .

**Income**

**Attach Form(s) W-2 here. Also attach Forms W-2G and 1099-R if tax was withheld.**

If you did not get a W-2, see page 22.

Enclose, but do not attach, any payment. Also, please use **Form 1040-V.**

7 Wages, salaries, tips, etc. Attach Form(s) W-2 . . . . . . . | 7
8a **Taxable** interest. Attach Schedule B if required . . . . . | 8a
b **Tax-exempt** interest. **Do not** include on line 8a . . . | 8b |
9a Ordinary dividends. Attach Schedule B if required . . . . | 9a
b Qualified dividends (see page 23) . . . . | 9b |
10 Taxable refunds, credits, or offsets of state and local income taxes (see page 23) . . | 10
11 Alimony received . . . . . . . . . . . . . . . . | 11
12 Business income or (loss). Attach Schedule C or C-EZ . . . . | 12
13 Capital gain or (loss). Attach Schedule D if required. If not required, check here ▶ ☐ | 13
14 Other gains or (losses). Attach Form 4797 . . . . . . . | 14
15a IRA distributions . . | 15a | b Taxable amount (see page 25) | 15b
16a Pensions and annuities | 16a | b Taxable amount (see page 25) | 16b
17 Rental real estate, royalties, partnerships, S corporations, trusts, etc. Attach Schedule E | 17
18 Farm income or (loss). Attach Schedule F . . . . . . . | 18
19 Unemployment compensation . . . . . . . . . . . | 19
20a Social security benefits . | 20a | b Taxable amount (see page 27) | 20b
21 Other income. List type and amount (see page 29) ---------------------- | 21
22 Add the amounts in the far right column for lines 7 through 21. This is your **total income** ▶ | 22

**Adjusted Gross Income**

23 Educator expenses (see page 29) . . . . . . | 23
24 Certain business expenses of reservists, performing artists, and fee-basis government officials. Attach Form 2106 or 2106-EZ | 24
25 Health savings account deduction. Attach Form 8889 . | 25
26 Moving expenses. Attach Form 3903 . . . . . | 26
27 One-half of self-employment tax. Attach Schedule SE . | 27
28 Self-employed SEP, SIMPLE, and qualified plans . . | 28
29 Self-employed health insurance deduction (see page 30) | 29
30 Penalty on early withdrawal of savings . . . . . | 30
31a Alimony paid    b Recipient's SSN ▶ _____ | 31a
32 IRA deduction (see page 31) . . . . . . . . | 32
33 Student loan interest deduction (see page 33) . . . | 33
34 Tuition and fees deduction (see page 34) . . . . | 34
35 Domestic production activities deduction. Attach Form 8903 | 35
36 Add lines 23 through 31a and 32 through 35 . . . . . . . . . . ▶ | 36
37 Subtract line 36 from line 22. This is your **adjusted gross income** . . . . . ▶ | 37

**For Disclosure, Privacy Act, and Paperwork Reduction Act Notice, see page 78.** Cat. No. 11320B Form **1040** (2005)

# Form 8 Form 1040

Form 1040 (2005)                                                                                            Page **2**

| | | | | |
|---|---|---|---|---|
| **Tax and Credits** | 38 | Amount from line 37 (adjusted gross income) . . . . . . . . . . | 38 | |

**39a** Check if: □ **You** were born before January 2, 1941, □ Blind. **Total boxes**
□ **Spouse** was born before January 2, 1941, □ Blind. checked ▶ **39a**

**Standard Deduction for—**

**b** If your spouse itemizes on a separate return or you were a dual-status alien, see page 35 and check here ▶**39b** □

**40** **Itemized deductions** (from Schedule A) **or your standard deduction** (see left margin) . . | **40** |

**41** Subtract line 40 from line 38 . . . . . . . . . . . . . . . . | **41** |

• People who checked any box on line 39a or 39b **or** who can be claimed as a dependent, see page 36.

**42** If line 38 is over $109,475, or you provided housing to a person displaced by Hurricane Katrina, see page 37. Otherwise, multiply $3,200 by the total number of exemptions claimed on line 6d | **42** |

**43** **Taxable income.** Subtract line 42 from line 41. If line 42 is more than line 41, enter -0- | **43** |

**44** **Tax** (see page 37). Check if any tax is from: **a** □ Form(s) 8814 **b** □ Form 4972 . . . | **44** |

• All others:

Single or Married filing separately, $5,000

**45** **Alternative minimum tax** (see page 39). Attach Form 6251 . . . . . . . | **45** |

**46** Add lines 44 and 45 . . . . . . . . . . . . . . . . . . ▶ | **46** |

Married filing jointly or Qualifying widow(er), $10,000

**47** Foreign tax credit. Attach Form 1116 if required | **47** |
**48** Credit for child and dependent care expenses. Attach Form 2441 | **48** |
**49** Credit for the elderly or the disabled. Attach Schedule R . . | **49** |

Head of household, $7,300

**50** Education credits. Attach Form 8863 . . . . . | **50** |
**51** Retirement savings contributions credit. Attach Form 8880 . | **51** |
**52** Child tax credit (see page 41). Attach Form 8901 if required | **52** |
**53** Adoption credit. Attach Form 8839 . . . . . | **53** |
**54** Credits from: **a** □ Form 8396 **b** □ Form 8859 . . | **54** |
**55** Other credits. Check applicable box(es): **a** □ Form 3800
**b** □ Form 8801 **c** □ Form _____ | **55** |

**56** Add lines 47 through 55. These are your **total credits** . . . . . . . | **56** |
**57** Subtract line 56 from line 46. If line 56 is more than line 46, enter -0-. . . . . ▶ | **57** |

| **Other Taxes** | |
|---|---|
| **58** Self-employment tax. Attach Schedule SE . . . . . . . . . | **58** |
| **59** Social security and Medicare tax on tip income not reported to employer. Attach Form 4137 . . | **59** |
| **60** Additional tax on IRAs, other qualified retirement plans, etc. Attach Form 5329 if required . | **60** |
| **61** Advance earned income credit payments from Form(s) W-2 . . . . . . . . | **61** |
| **62** Household employment taxes. Attach Schedule H . . . . . . . . | **62** |
| **63** Add lines 57 through 62. This is your **total tax** . . . . . . . . ▶ | **63** |

| **Payments** | |
|---|---|
| **64** Federal income tax withheld from Forms W-2 and 1099 . . | **64** |
| **65** 2005 estimated tax payments and amount applied from 2004 return | **65** |
| **66a** **Earned income credit (EIC)** . . . . . . . | **66a** |

If you have a qualifying child, attach Schedule EIC.

**b** Nontaxable combat pay election ▶ **66b**
**67** Excess social security and tier 1 RRTA tax withheld (see page 59) | **67** |
**68** Additional child tax credit. Attach Form 8812 . . . . . | **68** |
**69** Amount paid with request for extension to file (see page 59) | **69** |
**70** Payments from: **a** □ Form 2439 **b** □ Form 4136 **c** □ Form 8885 | **70** |
**71** Add lines 64, 65, 66a, and 67 through 70. These are your **total payments** . . . . ▶ | **71** |

| **Refund** | |
|---|---|
| **72** If line 71 is more than line 63, subtract line 63 from line 71. This is the amount you **overpaid** | **72** |
| **73a** Amount of line 72 you want **refunded to you** . . . . . . . . . . ▶ | **73a** |

Direct deposit? See page 59 and fill in 73b, 73c, and 73d.

▶ **b** Routing number ▶ **c** Type: □ Checking □ Savings
▶ **d** Account number
**74** Amount of line 72 you want **applied to your 2006 estimated tax** ▶ **74**

| **Amount You Owe** | |
|---|---|
| **75** **Amount you owe.** Subtract line 71 from line 63. For details on how to pay, see page 60 ▶ | **75** |
| **76** Estimated tax penalty (see page 60) . . . . . . . . . **76** | |

**Third Party Designee**

Do you want to allow another person to discuss this return with the IRS (see page 61)? □ **Yes.** Complete the following. □ **No**

Designee's name ▶        Phone no. ▶ (   )        Personal identification number (PIN) ▶

**Sign Here**

Under penalties of perjury, I declare that I have examined this return and accompanying schedules and statements, and to the best of my knowledge and belief, they are true, correct, and complete. Declaration of preparer (other than taxpayer) is based on all information of which preparer has any knowledge.

Joint return? See page 17. Keep a copy for your records.

Your signature | Date | Your occupation | Daytime phone number ( )
Spouse's signature. If a joint return, **both** must sign. | Date | Spouse's occupation |

**Paid Preparer's Use Only**

Preparer's signature ▶ | Date | Check if self-employed □ | Preparer's SSN or PTIN
Firm's name (or yours if self-employed), address, and ZIP code ▶ | EIN | Phone no. ( )

Form **1040** (2005)

✳ Printed on recycled paper

# Form 9 Form 1040A

| Form **1040A** | Department of the Treasury—Internal Revenue Service<br>**U.S. Individual Income Tax Return** (99) **2005** | | IRS Use Only—Do not write or staple in this space. |
|---|---|---|---|

**Label** (See page 18.)

**Use the IRS label.** Otherwise, please print or type.

L A B E L / H E R E

| Your first name and initial | Last name | | OMB No. 1545-0074 |
|---|---|---|---|

**Your social security number**

| If a joint return, spouse's first name and initial | Last name |
|---|---|

**Spouse's social security number**

| Home address (number and street). If you have a P.O. box, see page 18. | Apt. no. |
|---|---|

▲ You **must** enter your SSN(s) above. ▲

| City, town or post office, state, and ZIP code. If you have a foreign address, see page 18. |
|---|

Checking a box below will not change your tax or refund.

**Presidential Election Campaign** ▶ Check here if you, or your spouse if filing jointly, want $3 to go to this fund (see page 18) ▶ ☐ **You** ☐ **Spouse**

**Filing status**
Check only one box.

1 ☐ Single
2 ☐ Married filing jointly (even if only one had income)
3 ☐ Married filing separately. Enter spouse's SSN above and full name here. ▶

4 ☐ Head of household (with qualifying person). (See page 19.) If the qualifying person is a child but not your dependent, enter this child's name here. ▶
5 ☐ Qualifying widow(er) with dependent child (see page 19)

**Exemptions**

If more than six dependents, see page 21.

6a ☐ **Yourself.** If someone can claim you as a dependent, **do not** check box 6a.
  b ☐ **Spouse**
  c **Dependents:**

| (1) First name    Last name | (2) Dependent's social security number | (3) Dependent's relationship to you | (4) ✓ if qualifying child for child tax credit (see page 21) |
|---|---|---|---|
| | | | ☐ |
| | | | ☐ |
| | | | ☐ |
| | | | ☐ |
| | | | ☐ |
| | | | ☐ |

Boxes checked on 6a and 6b ___
No. of children on 6c who:
• lived with you ___
• did not live with you due to divorce or separation (see page 22) ___
Dependents on 6c not entered above ___
Add numbers on lines above ▶ ☐

  d Total number of exemptions claimed.

**Income**

**Attach Form(s) W-2 here. Also attach Form(s) 1099-R if tax was withheld.**

If you did not get a W-2, see page 24.

Enclose, but do not attach, any payment.

| 7 | Wages, salaries, tips, etc. Attach Form(s) W-2. | | 7 | |
|---|---|---|---|---|
| 8a | **Taxable** interest. Attach Schedule 1 if required. | | 8a | |
| b | **Tax-exempt** interest. **Do not** include on line 8a. | 8b | | |
| 9a | Ordinary dividends. Attach Schedule 1 if required. | | 9a | |
| b | Qualified dividends (see page 25). | 9b | | |
| 10 | Capital gain distributions (see page 25). | | 10 | |

| 11a | IRA distributions. 11a | 11b | Taxable amount (see page 25). | 11b |
|---|---|---|---|---|
| 12a | Pensions and annuities. 12a | 12b | Taxable amount (see page 26). | 12b |

| 13 | Unemployment compensation and Alaska Permanent Fund dividends. | | 13 | |
|---|---|---|---|---|

| 14a | Social security benefits. 14a | 14b | Taxable amount (see page 28). | 14b |
|---|---|---|---|---|

| 15 | Add lines 7 through 14b (far right column). This is your **total income.** ▶ | | 15 | |
|---|---|---|---|---|

**Adjusted gross income**

| 16 | Educator expenses (see page 28). | 16 | |
|---|---|---|---|
| 17 | IRA deduction (see page 28). | 17 | |
| 18 | Student loan interest deduction (see page 31). | 18 | |
| 19 | Tuition and fees deduction (see page 32). | 19 | |
| 20 | Add lines 16 through 19. These are your **total adjustments.** | | 20 |
| 21 | Subtract line 20 from line 15. This is your **adjusted gross income.** ▶ | | 21 |

**For Disclosure, Privacy Act, and Paperwork Reduction Act Notice, see page 58.**   Cat. No. 11327A   Form **1040A** (2005)

# Form 9 Form 1040A

| | | |
|---|---|---|
| **Tax, credits, and payments** | **22** Enter the amount from line 21 (adjusted gross income). | 22 |

**Standard Deduction for—**

• People who checked any box on line 23a or 23b **or** who can be claimed as a dependent, see page 32.

• All others:

Single or Married filing separately, $5,000

Married filing jointly or Qualifying widow(er), $10,000

Head of household, $7,300

**23a** Check if: □ **You** were born before January 2, 1941, □ Blind ⎱ **Total boxes**
□ **Spouse** was born before January 2, 1941, □ Blind ⎰ **checked** ▶ 23a ☐

**b** If you are married filing separately and your spouse itemizes deductions, see page 32 and check here ▶ 23b ☐

**24** Enter your **standard deduction** (see left margin). — 24

**25** Subtract line 24 from line 22. If line 24 is more than line 22, enter -0-. — 25

**26** If line 22 is over $109,475, or you provided housing to a person displaced by Hurricane Katrina, see page 33. Otherwise, multiply $3,200 by the total number of exemptions claimed on line 6d. — 26

**27** Subtract line 26 from line 25. If line 26 is more than line 25, enter -0-. This is your **taxable income.** ▶ 27

**28** **Tax,** including any alternative minimum tax (see page 34). — 28

**29** Credit for child and dependent care expenses. Attach Schedule 2. — 29

**30** Credit for the elderly or the disabled. Attach Schedule 3. — 30

**31** Education credits. Attach Form 8863. — 31

**32** Retirement savings contributions credit. Attach Form 8880. — 32

**33** Child tax credit (see page 38). Attach Form 8901 if required. — 33

**34** Adoption credit. Attach Form 8839. — 34

**35** Add lines 29 through 34. These are your **total credits.** — 35

**36** Subtract line 35 from line 28. If line 35 is more than line 28, enter -0-. — 36

**37** Advance earned income credit payments from Form(s) W-2. — 37

**38** Add lines 36 and 37. This is your **total tax.** ▶ 38

**39** Federal income tax withheld from Forms W-2 and 1099. — 39

**40** 2005 estimated tax payments and amount applied from 2004 return. — 40

If you have a qualifying child, attach Schedule EIC.

**41a** **Earned income credit (EIC).** — 41a

**b** Nontaxable combat pay election. 41b

**42** Additional child tax credit. Attach Form 8812. — 42

**43** Add lines 39, 40, 41a, and 42. These are your **total payments.** ▶ 43

**Refund**

Direct deposit? See page 53 and fill in 45b, 45c, and 45d.

**44** If line 43 is more than line 38, subtract line 38 from line 43. This is the amount you **overpaid.** — 44

**45a** Amount of line 44 you want **refunded to you.** ▶ 45a

▶ **b** Routing number [ ][ ][ ][ ][ ][ ][ ][ ][ ] ▶ **c** Type: ☐ Checking ☐ Savings

▶ **d** Account number [ ][ ][ ][ ][ ][ ][ ][ ][ ][ ][ ][ ][ ][ ][ ][ ][ ]

**46** Amount of line 44 you want **applied to your 2006 estimated tax.** — 46

**Amount you owe**

**47** **Amount you owe.** Subtract line 43 from line 38. For details on how to pay, see page 54. ▶ 47

**48** Estimated tax penalty (see page 54). — 48

**Third party designee**

Do you want to allow another person to discuss this return with the IRS (see page 55)? ☐ **Yes.** Complete the following. ☐ No

Designee's name ▶ _____ Phone no. ▶ ( ) _____ Personal identification number (PIN) ▶ [ ][ ][ ][ ][ ]

**Sign here**

Joint return? See page 18.

Keep a copy for your records.

Under penalties of perjury, I declare that I have examined this return and accompanying schedules and statements, and to the best of my knowledge and belief, they are true, correct, and accurately list all amounts and sources of income I received during the tax year. Declaration of preparer (other than the taxpayer) is based on all information of which the preparer has any knowledge.

Your signature | Date | Your occupation | Daytime phone number ( )

Spouse's signature. If a joint return, **both** must sign. | Date | Spouse's occupation

**Paid preparer's use only**

Preparer's signature ▶ | Date | Check if self-employed ☐ | Preparer's SSN or PTIN

Firm's name (or yours if self-employed), address, and ZIP code ▶ | EIN
Phone no. ( )

Form **1040A** (2005)

# Form 10 Form 1040EZ

Form
**1040EZ**

Department of the Treasury—Internal Revenue Service

**Income Tax Return for Single and Joint Filers With No Dependents** (99) **2005**

OMB No. 1545-0074

**Label**
(See page 11.)
**Use the IRS label.**
Otherwise, please print or type.

L A B E L

H E R E

| Your first name and initial | Last name | | Your social security number |
|---|---|---|---|
| If a joint return, spouse's first name and initial | Last name | | Spouse's social security number |
| Home address (number and street). If you have a P.O. box, see page 11. | | Apt. no. | ▲ You **must** enter ▲ your SSN(s) above. |
| City, town or post office, state, and ZIP code. If you have a foreign address, see page 11. | | | Checking a box below will not change your tax or refund. |

**Presidential Election Campaign** (page 12) ▶

Check here if you, or your spouse if a joint return, want $3 to go to this fund? . . . ▶ ☐ **You**    ☐ **Spouse**

**Income**

**Attach Form(s) W-2 here.**
Enclose, but do not attach, any payment.

**1** Wages, salaries, and tips. This should be shown in box 1 of your Form(s) W-2. Attach your Form(s) W-2. ⟶ **1**

**2** Taxable interest. If the total is over $1,500, you cannot use Form 1040EZ. ⟶ **2**

**3** Unemployment compensation and Alaska Permanent Fund dividends (see page 13). ⟶ **3**

**4** Add lines 1, 2, and 3. This is your **adjusted gross income.** ⟶ **4**

**5** If someone can claim you (or your spouse if a joint return) as a dependent, check the applicable box(es) below and enter the amount from the worksheet on back.
☐ **You**    ☐ **Spouse**
If someone cannot claim you (or your spouse if a joint return), enter $8,200 if **single**; $16,400 if **married filing jointly.** See back for explanation. ⟶ **5**

**6** Subtract line 5 from line 4. If line 5 is larger than line 4, enter -0-. This is your **taxable income.** ▶ **6**

**Payments and tax**

**7** Federal income tax withheld from box 2 of your Form(s) W-2. ⟶ **7**

**8a** **Earned income credit (EIC).** ⟶ **8a**

**b** Nontaxable combat pay election. **8b**

**9** Add lines 7 and 8a. These are your **total payments.** ▶ **9**

**10** **Tax.** Use the amount on **line 6 above** to find your tax in the tax table on pages 24–32 of the booklet. Then, enter the tax from the table on this line. ⟶ **10**

**Refund**

Have it directly deposited! See page 18 and fill in 11b, 11c, and 11d.

**11a** If line 9 is larger than line 10, subtract line 10 from line 9. This is your **refund.** ▶ **11a**

▶ **b** Routing number              ▶ **c** Type: ☐ Checking  ☐ Savings

▶ **d** Account number

**Amount you owe**

**12** If line 10 is larger than line 9, subtract line 9 from line 10. This is the **amount you owe.** For details on how to pay, see page 19. ▶ **12**

**Third party designee**

Do you want to allow another person to discuss this return with the IRS (see page 19)? ☐ **Yes.** Complete the following. ☐ **No**

Designee's name ▶            Phone no. ▶ (    )            Personal identification number (PIN) ▶

**Sign here**

Joint return? See page 11.
Keep a copy for your records.

Under penalties of perjury, I declare that I have examined this return, and to the best of my knowledge and belief, it is true, correct, and accurately lists all amounts and sources of income I received during the tax year. Declaration of preparer (other than the taxpayer) is based on all information of which the preparer has any knowledge.

| Your signature | Date | Your occupation | Daytime phone number |
|---|---|---|---|
| | | | (    ) |
| Spouse's signature. If a joint return, **both** must sign. | Date | Spouse's occupation | |

**Paid preparer's use only**

| Preparer's signature ▶ | | Date | Check if self-employed ☐ | Preparer's SSN or PTIN |
|---|---|---|---|---|
| Firm's name (or yours if self-employed), address, and ZIP code ▶ | | | EIN | |
| | | | Phone no. ( ) | |

For Disclosure, Privacy Act, and Paperwork Reduction Act Notice, see page 23.    Cat. No. 11329W    Form **1040EZ** (2005)

# Form 10 Form 1040EZ

| | |
|---|---|
| **Use this form if** | • Your filing status is single or married filing jointly. If you are not sure about your filing status, see page 11. |
| | • You (and your spouse if married filing jointly) were under age 65 and not blind at the end of 2005. If you were born on January 1, 1941, you are considered to be age 65 at the end of 2005. |
| | • You do not claim any dependents. For information on dependents, use TeleTax topic 354 (see page 6). |
| | • Your taxable income (line 6) is less than $100,000. |
| | • You do not claim any adjustments to income. For information on adjustments to income, use TeleTax topics 451-458 (see page 6). |
| | • The only tax credit you can claim is the earned income credit. For information on credits, use TeleTax topics 601-608 and 610 (see page 6). |
| | • You had only wages, salaries, tips, taxable scholarship or fellowship grants, unemployment compensation, or Alaska Permanent Fund dividends, and your taxable interest was not over $1,500. But if you earned tips, including allocated tips, that are not included in box 5 and box 7 of your Form W-2, you may not be able to use Form 1040EZ (see page 12). If you are planning to use Form 1040EZ for a child who received Alaska Permanent Fund dividends, see page 13. |
| | • You did not receive any advance earned income credit payments. If you cannot use this form, use TeleTax topic 352 (see page 6). |

| | |
|---|---|
| **Filling in your return**<br><br>For tips on how to avoid common mistakes, see page 20. | If you received a scholarship or fellowship grant or tax-exempt interest income, such as on municipal bonds, see the booklet before filling in the form. Also, see the booklet if you received a Form 1099-INT showing federal income tax withheld or if federal income tax was withheld from your unemployment compensation or Alaska Permanent Fund dividends.<br><br>Remember, you must report all wages, salaries, and tips even if you do not get a Form W-2 from your employer. You must also report all your taxable interest, including interest from banks, savings and loans, credit unions, etc., even if you do not get a Form 1099-INT. |

| | |
|---|---|
| **Worksheet for dependents who checked one or both boxes on line 5**<br><br>(keep a copy for your records) | Use this worksheet to figure the amount to enter on line 5 if someone can claim you (or your spouse if married filing jointly) as a dependent, even if that person chooses not to do so. To find out if someone can claim you as a dependent, use TeleTax topic 354 (see page 6).<br><br>**A.** Amount, if any, from line 1 on front . . . . . . . . . . . **A.** _____<br>**B.** Is line A more than $550?<br>  ☐ **Yes.** Add $250 to line A. Enter the total. ⎱ . . . . . . . . **B.** _____<br>  ☐ **No.** Enter $800. ⎰<br>**C.** If **single,** enter $5,000; if **married filing jointly,** enter $10,000 . . **C.** _____<br>**D.** Enter the **smaller** of line B or line C here. This is your standard deduction . . . . . . . . . . . . . . . . . . . **D.** _____<br>**E.** Exemption amount.<br>  • If single, enter -0-.<br>  • If married filing jointly and you checked—   ⎱<br>    —both boxes on line 5, enter -0-.   ⎰ **E.** _____<br>    —only one box on line 5, enter $3,200.<br>**F.** Add lines D and E. Enter the total here and on line 5 on the front . **F.** _____<br>**If you did not check any boxes on line 5,** enter on line 5 the amount shown below that applies to you.<br>• Single, enter $8,200. This is the total of your standard deduction ($5,000) and your exemption ($3,200).<br>• Married filing jointly, enter $16,400. This is the total of your standard deduction ($10,000), your exemption ($3,200), and your spouse's exemption ($3,200). |

| | |
|---|---|
| **Mailing return** | Mail your return by **April 17, 2006.** Use the envelope that came with your booklet. If you do not have that envelope or if you moved during the year, see the back cover for the address to use. |

Form **1040EZ** (2005)

# Form 11 Jury Summons Questionnaire

THE FOLLOWING "JUROR QUESTIONNAIRE" IS MANDATED BY GOVERNMENT CODE, SECTION 62.0132. YOUR ANSWERS ARE CONFIDENTIAL AND MAY BE DISCLOSED ONLY TO THE JUDGE, COURT PERSONNEL, THE LITIGANT, AND THE LITIGANT'S ATTORNEY. PLEASE TYPE OR PRINT WITH INK ONLY.

Your Name:

Home Address:

Mailing Address (if different from home):

County of Residence:                                                    How long have you lived in this county?

☐ –Male   ☐ –Female   Date of Birth:          Age:          Race (required by state law):          Are you a U.S. Citizen?  Y  N

Your Occupation:

Your Employer:                          How Long?          Prior Employer:                          How long?

If you are retired, prior occupation:                     If spouse retired, prior occupation:

Spouse's Name:                                             Spouse's occupation:

Spouse's Employer:                                                                          How long?

Current Marital Status: ☐–Single ☐–Married ☐–Widowed ☐–Divorced   Number of Children:   Range of Ages: from ___ years to ___ years

Occupation of Children:

Please check highest level of education completed:
☐–Did not receive H.S. Diploma ☐–H.S. Diploma ☐–GED ☐–2yr. College ☐–4 yr. College ☐–Post-Graduate ☐–Other:

Where did you grow up?          In what areas or activities do you have special knowledge or skills?

Other than your occupation, what are your activities or hobbies?

Have you ever served on a civil jury?  Y  N          Have you ever served on a criminal jury?  Y  N          Was a verdict reached?  Y  N

Have you ever been a party to a civil law suit?  Y  N          If yes, what type?

Have you ever sustained an injury requiring medical attention?  Y  N   If yes, describe your injury:

Has your spouse or any child ever sustained an injury requiring medical attention?  Y  N   If yes, describe the injury:
☐ –Spouse                                                            ☐ –Child

Have any relatives ever been a law enforcement officer?  Y  N   If yes, relation to you:          What type of officer?

Have you ever been ☐ –an accused, or ☐ –a complainant, or ☐ –a witness   in a criminal case?  Y  N

Your religious preference:                                    Service or civic organizations:

I certify that all answers are true and correct (please sign):

---

Social Security #:

Home Phone #:

Other Phone/Pager #:

Work Phone #:

# Form 12 Accident Report Form

## DIAGRAM

Draw detail sketch of accident on grid area. Show direction and position of vehicles involved. Show number of lanes, traffic control, pedestrians, etc. Use symbols shown below.

Your Vehicle

Other Vehicle(s)

Pedestrian

○ Stop Sign

□ Semaphore

▷ Yield

✕ Railroad

INDICATE NORTH BY ARROW

## BRIEF DESCRIPTION OF ACCIDENT

*(Tell how it happened, include length and positions of skid marks, etc.)*

## ACCIDENT INFORMATION

Date _____ Time _____ AM PM

Location _____
(STREET, HIGHWAY, ETC.)

_____ _____
(CITY) (STATE)

**WEATHER**
☐ Clear ☐ Raining ☐ Snowing
☐ Fog ☐ Sleeting
☐ Other _____

**AREA**
☐ Residential ☐ Commercial ☐ Rural
☐ Other _____

**PAVEMENT**
☐ Asphalt ☐ Concrete ☐ Gravel
☐ Other _____
Condition: ☐ Dry ☐ Wet ☐ Slippery
☐ Other _____

**DIRECTION**  N  E  S  W  OTHER
Yours  ☐  ☐  ☐  ☐  _____
Other  ☐  ☐  ☐  ☐  _____

**SPEED**  POSTED  ACTUAL
Yours  _____
Other  _____

**If Intersection — How Controlled**
☐ Not Controlled  ☐ Signal Light
☐ Stop Sign:
☐ 4 Way  ☐ three way  ☐ two way
☐ Other

# Form 12 Accident Report Form

## ACCIDENT REPORT

My Name _____

My Driver's License _____ (STATE)

My Employee No. (if known) _____

My Vehicle _____
(YEAR)     (MAKE)     (UNIT NO.)

_____
(LICENSE NO.)     (STATE)

Type of Vehicle _____

☐ Employer Owned    ☐ Privately Owned

☐ Business Use    ☐ Personal Use

### Insurance Identification

Policy No. _____

Insured's Name _____

Emergency Phone No. _____

Police Officer _____

Badge No. _____

Headquarters _____
(CITY, STATE & ZIP CODE)

Police Report made   ☐ Yes   ☐ No

## WITNESSES

1. Name _____
   Address _____
   Phone No. _____

2. Name _____
   Address _____
   Phone No. _____

3. Name _____
   Address _____
   Phone No. _____

4. Name _____
   Address _____
   Phone No. _____

5. Name _____
   Address _____
   Phone No. _____

## PERSONAL INJURIES

1. Name _____
   Address _____
   Injury _____

2. Name _____
   Address _____
   Injury _____

3. Name _____
   Address _____
   Injury _____

4. Name _____
   Address _____
   Injury _____
   Where taken after accident _____

## PROPERTY DAMAGE
(to property of others)

Owner _____

Address _____

Description of Damage _____

Make of Other Car _____

License Number _____

Driver's Name _____

Driver's Address _____

# Form 13 Apartment Lease Application

## Application for Occupancy

### 1. Personal (please print)

| Applicant | Daytime phone ( ) | Date of birth |
|---|---|---|
| Social security number | Driver's license number | |
| Spouse's name | Daytime phone ( ) | Date of birth |
| Spouse's social security number | Driver's license number | |

Apartment #
_____

Move-in
_____

Rental Amount
_____

Lease Term
_____

### 2. Employment (last 2 years)

| Present employer name | Telephone ( ) | | |
|---|---|---|---|
| Street address | City | State | Zip |
| How long employed | Monthly income | Position | Supervisor |
| Previous employer name | Telephone ( ) | | |
| Street address | City | State | Zip |
| How long employed | Monthly income | Position | Supervisor |
| Spouse's current employer name | Telephone ( ) | | |
| Street address | City | State | Zip |
| How long employed | Monthly income | Position | Supervisor |

Social security & pension benefits

### 3. Banking information

| Checking account bank name | |
|---|---|
| Checking account number | |
| Savings account bank name | |
| Savings account number | |

### 4. Residence history

| Present address | | | |
|---|---|---|---|
| City | State | Zip | Landlord's telephone ( ) |
| Present landlord (If owned home, show mortgage company) | How long | Monthly payment | Reason for leaving |
| Previous address | | | |
| City | State | Zip | Landlord's telephone ( ) |
| Previous landlord (If owned home, show mortgage company) | How long | Monthly payment | Reason for leaving |

### 5. Transportation

| Make and model of auto |
|---|
| Year |
| Tag Number |
| Color |
| County |
| State |
| Make and model of auto |
| Year |
| Tag number |
| Color |
| County |
| State |

### 6. Background

Have you or any occupant listed above ever :
(to answer "no" don't check block)

☐ been evicted or asked to move out?

☐ broken a rental agreement or apartment lease?

☐ declared bankruptcy?

☐ been sued for nonpayment of rent?

☐ been sued for damage to rental property?

☐ been convicted of a felony?

# Form 13 Apartment Lease Application

### 7. Other occupants

1.

| Relationship | Date of birth | Sex |
|---|---|---|

2.

| Relationship | Date of birth | Sex |
|---|---|---|

3.

| Relationship | Date of birth | Sex |
|---|---|---|

4.

| Relationship | Date of birth | Sex |
|---|---|---|

Number of persons who
will occupy apartment

Do you have any pets? If so, please specify
(type, breed, adult weight)

### 8. Referral

Who may we thank for referring you?
_____

Name of rental agency or locator service _____

_____

Agent's name _____

Friend (name) _____

Newspaper (name) _____

Other _____

_____

### 9. Emergency

In an emergency, notify (preferably a relative)
Name _____

Address _____

Work phone (     ) _____

Home phone (     ) _____

E-Mail _____

Relationship _____

This person does (    ) does not (    ) have permission
to enter my apartment in an emergency.

I/We have submitted the sum of $_____ non-refundable payment for a credit check and processing charge, receipt of which is acknowledged by management. Such sum should not be considered rental payment, security deposit, or payment of administrative fee. In the event this application is disapproved, this sum will be retained by management to cover the cost of processing this application as furnished by me. I certify that the information given herein is complete, true and correct. I or we authorize you to verify all information on my rental application by all available means, including consumer reporting agencies, public records, current and previous rental property owners and managers, employers and personal references. Reverification or investigation of preliminary findings is not required.

I/We hereby deposit $_____ with Management as a good faith deposit in connection with this rental application. If my application is accepted, I understand this deposit will be applied toward payment of my security deposit of $_____ which is due in full prior to taking possession of the apartment. If Management accepts my application, I agree to execute Management's usual rental agreement on or before the occupancy date set out in this application. If for any reason Management decides to decline this application, then Management will refund this good faith deposit to me in full. I understand I may cancel this application by written notice within 72 hours and receive a full refund of this good faith deposit. I understand that if my good faith deposit is paid in cash or money order that it may take up to 30 days for me to receive a refund if I cancel within 72 hours or if my application is denied. If I fail to cancel within 72 hours and fail to execute Manager's usual rental agreement, or refuse to occupy the premises on the agreed upon date, the deposit of all applicants will be retained by owner as liquidated damages and the parties shall have no further obligation to each other. Applicant further agrees that the signing of this application does not constitute an obligation on the part of the landlord to provide an apartment until the signing of landlord lease agreement by both parties. I, the undersigned, hereby acknowledge that I have read, fully understand, and agree to the above terms and conditions.

By signing this application, I/we declare that all of my/our responses are true and complete and authorize owner to verify this information. I understand that any false statement made on this application can, among other responses, lead to rejection of my application or the immediate termination of my lease.

Applicant's Signature

Date:

Spouse's Signature

Date:

Consultant

Date:

# Form 14 Passport Application

## U.S. Department of State
## APPLICATION FOR A US PASSPORT

OMB APPROVAL NO. 1405-0004
EXPIRATION DATE: 08/31/2008
ESTIMATED BURDEN: 85 Minutes
(See Instruction Page 3)

**WARNING:** False statements made knowingly and willfully in passport applications, including affidavits or other supporting documents submitted therewith, are punishable by fine and/or imprisonment under provisions of 18 U.S.C. 1001, 18 U.S.C. 1542 and/or 18 U.S.C. 1621. Alteration or mutilation of a passport issued pursuant to this application is punishable by fine and/or imprisonment under the provisions of 18 U.S.C 1543. The use of a passport in violation of the restrictions contained therein or of the passport regulations is punishable by fine and/or imprisonment under 18 U.S.C. 1544. All statements and documents are subject to verification.

☐ 5 Yr. ☐ 10 Yr. **Issue Date** _____

☐ R ☐ D ☐ O ☐ DP

End. # _____ Exp. _____

When completing this form, PRINT IN BLUE OR BLACK INK ONLY

### 1. Name of Applicant

| Last | | Suffix (Jr., Sr., III) |
|---|---|---|
| First | | Middle |

### 2. Date of Birth (mm-dd-yyyy)

| 3. Sex | 4. Place of Birth (City & State OR City & Country) | 5. Social Security Number (See Federal Tax Law Notice on Instruction Page 3) | 6. Alien Registration No. (If applicable) |
|---|---|---|---|
| ☐ M ☐ F | | | |

| 7. Height | 8. Hair Color | 9. Eye Color | 10. Occupation | 11. Employer |
|---|---|---|---|---|
| Feet Inches | | | | |

### 12. E-Mail Address (Optional)

### 13. Mailing Address

| Street/RFD# **OR** Post Office Box | | Apartment # |
|---|---|---|
| City | State | ZIP Code |
| Country (If outside the U.S.) | In Care of (If applicable) | |

FROM 1" TO 1 3/8"

2" x 2"    2" x 2"

Submit two recent, color photographs

### 14. Permanent Address or Residence (If same as mailing address write "Same As Above")

| Street / RFD # (DO NOT LIST P.O. BOX) | | Apartment # |
|---|---|---|
| City | State | ZIP Code |

| 15. Home Telephone (Include Area Code) | 16. Business Telephone (Include Area Code) |
|---|---|
| ( ) | ( ) |

### 17. Have you ever applied for <u>or</u> been issued a U.S. passport?

☐ YES ☐ NO

If yes, complete the remaining items in block #17 and submit most recent passport.

| Name in which your most recent passport was issued. | Status of recent passport ☐ Submitted ☐ Stolen ☐ Lost ☐ Other |
|---|---|
| Most recent passport number. | Approximate date your most recent U.S. passport was issued or date (mm-dd-yyyy) you applied. |

### 18. Travel Plans

| Date of Trip (mm-dd-yyyy) | Length of Trip | Countries to be Visited |
|---|---|---|

### 19. Have you ever been married? ☐ YES ☐ NO    If yes, complete the remaining items in block #19

| Spouse's or Former Spouse's Full Name | Is your spouse (or former spouse) a U.S. citizen? ☐ YES ☐ NO |
|---|---|
| Date of Birth (mm-dd-yyyy) | Place of Birth | Date of Most Recent Marriage | Widowed? ☐ Divorced? ☐ Give Date: |

### 20. What other names have you used? (Include name changes, maiden name, & former married names)

| 1) | 2) | 3) | 4) |
|---|---|---|---|

DS-11
09-2005

DS 11 06 2005

Page 1 of 2

# Form 14 Passport Application

| NAME OF APPLICANT (Last, First, Middle) | | | | Date of Birth *(mm-dd-yyyy)* | |
|---|---|---|---|---|---|

**21. Parental Information**

| Mother's Maiden Name | | | | Date of Birth | Place of Birth |
|---|---|---|---|---|---|
| Last | First | | Middle | | |

| Father's Name | | | | Date of Birth | Place of Birth |
|---|---|---|---|---|---|
| Last | First | | Middle | | |

| Is your mother a U.S. citizen? | ☐ YES ☐ NO | Is your father a U.S. citizen? | ☐ YES ☐ NO |
|---|---|---|---|

**22. Emergency Contact** - Provide the information of a person not traveling with you to be contacted in the event of an emergency.

| Name | | Street / RFD # | |
|---|---|---|---|
| Apartment # | City | State | ZIP Code |
| Telephone ( ) | E-Mail Address *(Optional)* | | Relationship |

**STOP** DO NOT SIGN APPLICATION UNTIL REQUESTED TO DO SO BY PERSON ADMINISTERING OATH.

**23. Oath & Signature**

I declare under penalty of perjury that I am a United States citizen (or non-citizen national) and have not, since acquiring United State citizenship (or U.S. nationality), performed any of the acts listed under "Acts or Conditions" on this application form (unless explanatory statement is attached). I declare under penalty that the statements made on this application are true and correct.

X _____
Applicant's Signature - age 14 and older

X _____
Mother's Legal Guardian's Signature *(If identifying minor)*

X _____
Father's Legal Guardian's Signature *(If identifying minor)*

**Applicant's or Father's Identification Information**

Type of Document     Issue Date _____
☐ Driver's License     Expiration Date _____
☐ Passport
☐ Military Identification     Place of Issue _____
☐ Other (Specify) _____

Name _____

ID Number _____

**Mother's Identification Information**

Type of Document     Issue Date _____
☐ Driver's License     Expiration Date _____
☐ Passport
☐ Military Identification     Place of Issue _____
☐ Other (Specify) _____

Name _____

ID Number _____

## FOR ACCEPTANCE AGENT USE ONLY

Facility Identification Number _____

☐ Acceptance Agent; Facility Name & Location
_____

☐ (Vice) Consul USA; Location
_____

☐ Passport Services Staff Agent
Subscribed & sworn to (affirmed) before me

_____ Date *(mm-dd-yyyy)* _____
(Signature of person authorized to accept application)

(SEAL)

**For Issuing Office Use Only**

Name as it appears on citizenship evidence _____

☐ Birth Certificate ☐ SR ☐ CR ☐ City    File Date _____ Issue Date _____

☐ Passport   Issue Date: _____

☐ Report of Birth ☐ 240 ☐ 545 ☐ 1350   Issue Date _____

☐ Naturalization Certificate   Issue Date _____ Cert. # _____

☐ Citizenship Certificate   Issue Date _____ Cert. # _____

☐ Other: _____

☐ Seen & Returned

☐ Attached _____

FEE _____ EXEC. _____ EF _____ OTHER _____

APPLICATION APPROVAL

DS-11

Page 2 of 2

# Form 15 Application for Immigrant Visa and Alien Registration

U.S. Department of State

OMB APPROVAL NO. 1405-0015
EXPIRES: 07/31/2007
ESTIMATED BURDEN: 1 HOUR*
(See Page 2)

## APPLICATION FOR IMMIGRANT VISA AND ALIEN REGISTRATION

### PART I - BIOGRAPHIC DATA

**INSTRUCTIONS:** Complete one copy of this form for yourself and each member of your family, regardless of age, who will immigrate with you. Please print or type your answers to all questions. Mark questions that are **Not Applicable** with "N/A". If there is insufficient room on the form, answer on a separate sheet using the same numbers that appear on the form. Attach any additional sheets to this form.

**WARNING:** Any false statement or concealment of a material fact may result in your permanent exclusion from the United States.

This form (DS-230 PART I) is the first of two parts. This part, together with Form DS-230 PART II, constitutes the complete Application for Immigrant Visa and Alien Registration.

| 1. Family Name | First Name | Middle Name |
|---|---|---|
| | | |

2. Other Names Used or Aliases *(If married woman, give maiden name)*

3. Full Name in Native Alphabet *(If Roman letters not used)*

Full Name in Native alphabet

| 4. Date of Birth *(mm-dd-yyyy)* | 5. Age | 6. Place of Birth |
|---|---|---|
| | | *(City or town)*          *(Province)*          *(Country)* |

| 7. Nationality *(If dual national, give both)* | 8. Gender | 9. Marital Status |
|---|---|---|
| | ☐ Male ☐ Female | ☐ Single *(Never married)*  ☐ Married  ☐ Widowed  ☐ Divorced  ☐ Separated<br>Including my present marriage, I have been married _____ times. |

| 10. Permanent address in the United States where you intend to live, if known *(street address including zip code)*. Include the name of a person who currently lives there.<br><br>Telephone number: | 11. Address in the United States where you want your Permanent Resident Card (Green Card) mailed, if different from address in item #10 *(include the name of a person who currently lives there)*.<br><br>Telephone number: |
|---|---|

| 12. Your Present Occupation | 13. Present Address *(Street Address) (City or Town) (Province) (Country)*<br><br>Telephone number:  Home                    Office |
|---|---|

14. Name of Spouse *(Maiden or family name)*          First Name          Middle Name

Date *(mm-dd-yyyy)* and place of birth of spouse:

Address of spouse *(If different from your own)*:

Spouse's occupation:          Date of marriage *(mm-dd-yyyy)*:

| 15. Father's Family Name | First Name | Middle Name |
|---|---|---|

| 16. Father's Date of Birth *(mm-dd-yyyy)* | Place of Birth | Current Address | If deceased, give year of death |
|---|---|---|---|

| 17. Mother's Family Name at Birth | First Name | Middle Name |
|---|---|---|

| 18. Mother's Date of Birth *(mm-dd-yyyy)* | Place of Birth | Current Address | If deceased, give year of death |
|---|---|---|---|

DS-230 Part I
07-2004

THIS FORM MAY BE OBTAINED FREE AT CONSULAR OFFICES OF THE UNITED STATES OF AMERICA
PREVIOUS EDITIONS OBSOLETE

Page 1 of 4

# Form 15 Application for Immigrant Visa and Alien Registration

**19.** List Names, Dates and Places of Birth, and Addresses of **ALL** Children.

| NAME | DATE *(mm-dd-yyyy)* | PLACE OF BIRTH | ADDRESS *(If different from your own)* |
|------|------|------|------|
| | | | |
| | | | |
| | | | |
| | | | |
| | | | |

**20.** List below all places you have lived for at least six months since reaching the age of 16, including places in your country of nationality. Begin with your present residence.

| CITY OR TOWN | PROVINCE | COUNTRY | FROM/TO *(mm-yyyy)* |
|------|------|------|------|
| | | | |
| | | | |
| | | | |
| | | | |
| | | | |

**21a.** Person(s) named in 14 and 19 who will accompany you to the United States now.

**21b.** Person(s) named in 14 and 19 who will follow you to the United States at a later date.

**22.** List below all employment for the last ten years.

| EMPLOYER | LOCATION | JOB TITLE | FROM/TO *(mm-yyyy)* |
|------|------|------|------|
| | | | |
| | | | |
| | | | |
| | | | |

In what occupation do you intend to work in the United States?_____

**23.** List below all educational institutions attended.

| SCHOOL AND LOCATION | FROM/TO *(mm-yyyy)* | COURSE OF STUDY | DEGREE OR DIPLOMA |
|------|------|------|------|
| | | | |
| | | | |
| | | | |

Languages spoken or read:_____

Professional associations to which you belong:_____

**24.** Previous Military Service ☐ Yes ☐ No

Branch:_____ Dates *(mm-dd-yyyy)* of Service:_____

Rank/Position:_____ Military Speciality/Occupation:_____

**25.** List dates of all previous visits to or residence in the United States. *(If never, write "never")* Give type of visa status, if known. Give DHS "A" number if any.

| FROM/TO *(mm-yyyy)* | LOCATION | TYPE OF VISA | "A" NO. *(If known)* |
|------|------|------|------|
| | | | |
| | | | |

SIGNATURE OF APPLICANT | DATE *(mm-dd-yyyy)*

**Privacy Act and Paperwork Reduction Act Statements**

The information asked for on this form is requested pursuant to Section 222 of the Immigration and Nationality Act. The U.S. Department of State uses the facts you provide on this form primarily to determine your classification and eligibility for a U.S. immigrant visa. Individuals who fail to submit this form or who do not provide all the requested information may be denied a U.S. immigrant visa. If you are issued an immigrant visa and are subsequently admitted to the United States as an immigrant, the Department of Homeland Security will use the information on this form to issue you a Permanent Resident Card, and, if you so indicate, the Social Security Administration will use the information to issue you a social security number and card.

*Public reporting burden for this collection of information is estimated to average 1 hour per response, including time required for searching existing data sources, gathering the necessary data, providing the information required, and reviewing the final collection. In accordance with 5 CFR 1320 5(b), persons are not required to respond to the collection of this information unless this form displays a currently valid OMB control number. Send comments on the accuracy of this estimate of the burden and recommendations for reducing it to: U.S. Department of State (A/RPS/DIR) Washington, DC 20520.

DS-230 Part I

Page 2 of 4

# Form 15 Application for Immigrant Visa and Alien Registration

U.S. Department of State

## APPLICATION FOR IMMIGRANT VISA AND ALIEN REGISTRATION

OMB APPROVAL NO. 1405-0015
EXPIRES: 07/31/2007
ESTIMATED BURDEN: 1 HOUR*

### PART II - SWORN STATEMENT

**INSTRUCTIONS:** Complete one copy of this form for yourself and each member of your family, regardless of age, who will immigrate with you. Please print or type your answers to all questions. Mark questions that are **Not Applicable** with **"N/A"**. If there is insufficient room on the form, answer on a separate sheet using the same numbers that appear on the form. Attach any additional sheets to this form. The fee should be paid in United States dollars or local currency equivalent, or by bank draft.

**WARNING:** Any false statement or concealment of a material fact may result in your permanent exclusion from the United States. Even if you are issued an immigrant visa and are subsequently admitted to the United States, providing false information on this form could be grounds for your prosecution and/or deportation.

This form (DS-230 PART II), together with Form DS-230 PART I, constitutes the complete Application for Immigrant Visa and Alien Registration.

| 26. Family Name | First Name | Middle Name |
|---|---|---|
| | | |

27. Other Names Used or Aliases *(If married woman, give maiden name)*

28. Full Name in Native Alphabet *(If Roman letters not used)*

29. Name and Address of Petitioner

Telephone number:

30. United States laws governing the issuance of visas require each applicant to state whether or not he or she is a member of any class of individuals excluded from admission into the United States. The excludable classes are described below in general terms. You should read carefully the following list and answer YES or NO to each category. The answers you give will assist the consular officer to reach a decision on your eligibility to receive a visa.

**EXCEPT AS OTHERWISE PROVIDED BY LAW, ALIENS WITHIN THE FOLLOWING CLASSIFICATIONS ARE INELIGIBLE TO RECEIVE A VISA.**
**DO ANY OF THE FOLLOWING CLASSES APPLY TO YOU?**

a. An alien who has a communicable disease of public health significance; who has failed to present documentation of having received vaccinations in accordance with U.S. law; who has or has had a physical or mental disorder that poses or is likely to pose a threat to the safety or welfare of the alien or others; or who is a drug abuser or addict. ☐ Yes ☐ No

b. An alien convicted of, or who admits having committed, a crime involving moral turpitude or violation of any law relating to a controlled substance or who is the spouse, son or daughter of such a trafficker who knowingly has benefited from the trafficking activities in the past five years; who has been convicted of 2 or more offenses for which the aggregate sentences were 5 years or more; who is coming to the United States to engage in prostitution or commercialized vice or who has engaged in prostitution or procuring within the past 10 years; who is or has been an illicit trafficker in any controlled substance; who has committed a serious criminal offense in the United States and who has asserted immunity from prosecution; who, while serving as a foreign government official and within the previous 24-month period, was responsible for or directly carried out particularly severe violations of religious freedom; or whom the President has identified as a person who plays a significant role in a severe form of trafficking in persons, who otherwise has knowingly aided, abetted, assisted or colluded with such a trafficker in severe forms of trafficking in persons, or who is the spouse, son or daughter of such a trafficker who knowingly has benefited from the trafficking activities within the past five years. ☐ Yes ☐ No

c. An alien who seeks to enter the United States to engage in espionage, sabotage, export control violations, terrorist activities, the overthrow of the Government of the United States or other unlawful activity; who is a member of or affiliated with the Communist or other totalitarian party; who participated in Nazi persecutions or genocide; who has engaged in genocide; or who is a member or representative of a terrorist organization as currently designated by the U.S. Secretary of State. ☐ Yes ☐ No

d. An alien who is likely to become a public charge. ☐ Yes ☐ No

e. An alien who seeks to enter for the purpose of performing skilled or unskilled labor who has not been certified by the Secretary of Labor; who is a graduate of a foreign medical school seeking to perform medical services who has not passed the NBME exam or its equivalent; or who is a health care worker seeking to perform such work without a certificate from the CGFNS or from an equivalent approved independent credentialing organization. ☐ Yes ☐ No

f. An alien who failed to attend a hearing on deportation or inadmissibility within the last 5 years; who seeks or has sought a visa, entry into the United States, or any immigration benefit by fraud or misrepresentation; who knowingly assisted any other alien to enter or try to enter the United States in violation of law; who, after November 30, 1996, attended in student (F) visa status a U.S. public elementary school or who attended a U.S. public secondary school without reimbursing the school; or who is subject to a civil penalty under INA 274C. ☐ Yes ☐ No

### Privacy Act and Paperwork Reduction Act Statements

The information asked for on this form is requested pursuant to Section 222 of the Immigration and Nationality Act. The U.S. Department of State uses the facts you provide on this form primarily to determine your classification and eligibility for a U.S. immigrant visa. Individuals who fail to submit this form or who do not provide all the requested information may be denied a U.S. immigrant visa. If you are issued an immigrant visa and are subsequently admitted to the United States as an immigrant, the Department of Homeland Security will use the information on this form to issue you a Permanent Resident Card, and, if you so indicate, the Social Security Administration will use the information to issue you a social security number and card.

*Public reporting burden for this collection of information is estimated to average 1 hour per response, including time required for searching existing data sources, gathering the necessary data, providing the information required, and reviewing the final collection. In accordance with 5 CFR 1320.5(b), persons are not required to respond to the collection of this information unless this form displays a currently valid OMB control number. Send comments on the accuracy of this estimate of the burden and recommendations for reducing it to: U.S. Department of State (A/RPS/DIR) Washington, DC 20520.

DS-230 Part II                    PREVIOUS EDITIONS OBSOLETE                    Page 3 of 4

# Form 15 Application for Immigrant Visa and Alien Registration

| | | Yes | No |
|---|---|---|---|
| g. | An alien who is permanently ineligible for U.S. citizenship; or who departed the United States to evade military service in time of war. | ☐ Yes | ☐ No |
| h. | An alien who was previously ordered removed within the last 5 years or ordered removed a second time within the last 20 years; who was previously unlawfully present and ordered removed within the last 10 years or ordered removed a second time within the last 20 years; who was convicted of an aggravated felony and ordered removed; who was previously unlawfully present in the United States for more than 180 days but less than one year who voluntarily departed within the last 3 years; or who was unlawfully present for more than one year or an aggregate of one year within the last 10 years. | ☐ Yes | ☐ No |
| i. | An alien who is coming to the United States to practice polygamy; who withholds custody of a U.S. citizen child outside the United States from a person granted legal custody by a U.S. court or intentionally assists another person to do so; who has voted in the United States in violation of any law or regulation; or who renounced U.S. citizenship to avoid taxation. | ☐ Yes | ☐ No |
| j. | An alien who is a former exchange visitor who has not fulfilled the 2-year foreign residence requirement. | ☐ Yes | ☐ No |
| k. | An alien determined by the Attorney General to have knowingly made a frivolous application for asylum. | ☐ Yes | ☐ No |
| l. | An alien who has ordered, carried out or materially assisted in extrajudicial and political killings and other acts of violence against the Haitian people; who has directly or indirectly assisted or supported any of the groups in Colombia known as FARC, ELN, or AUC; who through abuse of a governmental or political position has converted for personal gain, confiscated or expropriated property in Cuba, a claim to which is owned by a national of the United States, has trafficked in such property or has been complicit in such conversion, has committed similar acts in another country, or is the spouse, minor child or agent of an alien who has committed such acts; who has been directly involved in the establishment or enforcement of population controls forcing a woman to undergo an abortion against her free choice or a man or a woman to undergo sterilization against his or her free choice; or who has disclosed or trafficked in confidential U.S. business information obtained in connection with U.S. participation in the Chemical Weapons Convention or is the spouse, minor child or agent of such a person. | ☐ Yes | ☐ No |

---

**31.** Have you ever been charged, arrested or convicted of any offense or crime?  ☐ Yes ☐ No
*(If answer is Yes, please explain)*

---

**32.** Have you ever been refused admission to the United States at a port-of-entry?  ☐ Yes ☐ No
*(If answer is Yes, please explain)*

---

**33a.** Have you ever applied for a Social Security Number (SSN)?

☐ Yes   Give the number _____   ☐ No

Do you want the Social Security Administration to assign you an SSN (and issue a card) or issue you a new card (if you have an SSN)? You must answer "Yes" to this question and to the "Consent To Disclosure" in order to receive an SSN and/or card.

☐ Yes   ☐ No

**33b. CONSENT TO DISCLOSURE:** I authorize disclosure of information from this form to the Department of Homeland Security (DHS), the Social Security Administration (SSA), such other U.S. Government agencies as may be required for the purpose of assigning me an SSN and issuing me a Social Security card, and I authorize the SSA to share my SSN with the INS.

☐ Yes   ☐ No

The applicant's response does not limit or restrict the Government's ability to obtain his or her SSN, or other information on this form, for enforcement or other purposes as authorized by law.

---

**34.** WERE YOU ASSISTED IN COMPLETING THIS APPLICATION? ☐ Yes ☐ No
*(If answer is Yes, give name and address of person assisting you, indicating whether relative, friend, travel agent, attorney, or other)*

---

**DO NOT WRITE BELOW THE FOLLOWING LINE**
The consular officer will assist you in answering item 35.
**DO NOT SIGN** this form until instructed to do so by the consular officer

---

**35.** I claim to be:

☐ A Family-Sponsored Immigrant
☐ An Employment-Based Immigrant
☐ A Diversity Immigrant
☐ A Special Category *(Specify)* _____
*(Returning resident, Hong Kong, Tibetan, Private Legislation, etc.)*

☐ I derive foreign state chargeability under Sec. 202(b) through my _____

☐ Preference: _____

☐ Numerical limitation: _____
*(foreign state)*

I understand that I am required to surrender my visa to the United States Immigration Officer at the place where I apply to enter the United States, and that the possession of a visa does not entitle me to enter the United States if at that time I am found to be inadmissible under the immigration laws.
I understand that any willfully false or misleading statement or willful concealment of a material fact made by me herein may subject me to permanent exclusion from the United States and, if I am admitted to the United States, may subject me to criminal prosecution and/or deportation.
I, the undersigned applicant for a United States immigrant visa, do solemnly swear (or affirm) that all statements which appear in this application, consisting of Form DS-230 Part I and Part II combined, have been made by me, including the answers to items 1 through 35 inclusive, and that they are true and complete to the best of my knowledge and belief. I do further swear (or affirm) that, if admitted into the United States, I will not engage in activities which would be prejudicial to the public interest, or endanger the welfare, safety, or security of the United States; in activities which would be prohibited by the laws of the United States relating to espionage, sabotage, public disorder, or in other activities subversive to the national security; in any activity a purpose of which is the opposition to, or the control, or overthrow of, the Government of the United States, by force, violence or other unconstitutional means.
I understand that completion of this form by persons required by law to register with the Selective Service System (males 18 through 25 years of age) constitutes such registration in accordance with the Military Selective Service Act.
I understand all the foregoing statements, having asked for and obtained an explanation on every point which was not clear to me.

_____
Signature of Applicant

Subscribed and sworn to before me this _____ day of _____ _____ at: _____

_____
Consular Officer

**THIS FORM MAY BE OBTAINED FREE AT CONSULAR OFFICES OF THE UNITED STATES OF AMERICA**

DS-230 Part II

Page 4 of 4

# Form 16 Social Security Card Application

## SOCIAL SECURITY ADMINISTRATION
## Application for a Social Security Card

Form Approved
OMB No. 0960-0066

**1**

| NAME TO BE SHOWN ON CARD → | First | Full Middle Name | Last |
|---|---|---|---|
| FULL NAME AT BIRTH IF OTHER THAN ABOVE | First | Full Middle Name | Last |
| OTHER NAMES USED | | | |

**2** MAILING ADDRESS Do Not Abbreviate →

Street Address, Apt. No., PO Box, Rural Route No.

| City | State | ZIP Code |
|---|---|---|
| | | - |

**3** CITIZENSHIP (Check One) →
☐ U.S. Citizen   ☐ Legal Alien Allowed To Work   ☐ Legal Alien Not Allowed To Work (See Instructions On Page 2)   ☐ Other (See Instructions On Page 2)

**4** SEX → ☐ Male   ☐ Female

**5** RACE/ETHNIC DESCRIPTION (Check One Only - Voluntary) →
☐ Asian, Asian-American or Pacific Islander   ☐ Hispanic   ☐ Black (Not Hispanic)   ☐ North American Indian or Alaskan Native   ☐ White (Not Hispanic)

**6** DATE OF BIRTH _____ Month, Day, Year

**7** PLACE OF BIRTH _____ (Do Not Abbreviate) City _____ State or Foreign Country _____ FCI

Office Use Only

**8**

A. MOTHER'S NAME AT HER BIRTH → First | Full Middle Name | Last Name At Her Birth

B. MOTHER'S SOCIAL SECURITY NUMBER (See instructions for 8B on Page 2) → ⎣⎦⎣⎦⎣⎦ - ⎣⎦⎣⎦ - ⎣⎦⎣⎦⎣⎦⎣⎦

**9**

A. FATHER'S NAME → First | Full Middle Name | Last

B. FATHER'S SOCIAL SECURITY NUMBER (See instructions for 9B on Page 2) → ⎣⎦⎣⎦⎣⎦ - ⎣⎦⎣⎦ - ⎣⎦⎣⎦⎣⎦⎣⎦

**10** Has the applicant or anyone acting on his/her behalf ever filed for or received a Social Security number card before?
☐ Yes (If "yes", answer questions 11-13.)   ☐ No (If "no," go on to question 14.)   ☐ Don't Know (If "don't know," go on to question 14.)

**11** Enter the Social Security number previously assigned to the person listed in item 1. → ⎣⎦⎣⎦⎣⎦ - ⎣⎦⎣⎦ - ⎣⎦⎣⎦⎣⎦⎣⎦

**12** Enter the name shown on the most recent Social Security card issued for the person listed in item 1. → First | Middle Name | Last

**13** Enter any different date of birth if used on an earlier application for a card. → _____ Month, Day, Year

**14** TODAY'S DATE _____ Month, Day, Year

**15** DAYTIME PHONE NUMBER ( ) - _____ Area Code   Number

I declare under penalty of perjury that I have examined all the information on this form, and on any accompanying statements or forms, and it is true and correct to the best of my knowledge.

**16** YOUR SIGNATURE ▶

**17** YOUR RELATIONSHIP TO THE PERSON IN ITEM 1 IS:
☐ Self   ☐ Natural Or Adoptive Parent   ☐ Legal Guardian   ☐ Other (Specify)

DO NOT WRITE BELOW THIS LINE (FOR SSA USE ONLY)

| NPN | | | DOC | NTI | CAN | | ITV |
|---|---|---|---|---|---|---|---|
| PBC | EVI | EVA | EVC | PRA | NWR | DNR | UNIT |

EVIDENCE SUBMITTED

SIGNATURE AND TITLE OF EMPLOYEE(S) REVIEWING EVIDENCE AND/OR CONDUCTING INTERVIEW

DATE

DCL   DATE

Form SS-5 (12-2005)   ef (12-2005)   Destroy Prior Editions   Page 5

# Form 17 Selective Service System Registration Form

*Register on-line (http://www*

## SELECTIVE SERVICE SYSTEM REGISTRATION FORM

PRINT ONLY IN BLACK INK AND IN CAPITAL LETTERS ONLY

**1 ▲** DATE OF BIRTH: (MM-DD-YYYY)

**2 ▲** SEX: (Mark with "X")  Male  Female

**3 ▲** SOCIAL SECURITY ACCOUNT NUMBER

SUFFIX: (Mark with "X")  JR  III  OTHER SUFFIX

**4 ▲** LAST NAME

FIRST NAME & MIDDLE NAME

**5 ▲** CURRENT MAILING ADDRESS: STREET ADDRESS & APARTMENT NUMBER

CITY  STATE  ZIP CODE

**6 ▲** TODAY'S DATE: (MM-DD-YYYY)

**7 ▲** I AFFIRM THE FOREGOING STATEMENTS ARE TRUE

SIGNATURE  UPO

DO NOT WRITE IN THIS SPACE

# Form 18 Patient's Request for Medical Payment

DEPARTMENT OF HEALTH AND HUMAN SERVICES
CENTERS FOR MEDICARE & MEDICAID SERVICES

FORM APPROVED
OMB NO 0938-0008

## PATIENT'S REQUEST FOR MEDICAL PAYMENT

### IMPORTANT – SEE OTHER SIDE FOR INSTRUCTIONS

PLEASE TYPE OR PRINT INFORMATION — MEDICAL INSURANCE BENEFITS SOCIAL SECURITY ACT

NOTICE: Anyone who misrepresents or falsifies essential information requested by this form may upon conviction be subject to fine and imprisonment under Federal law. No Part B Medicare benefits may be paid unless this form is received as required by existing law and regulations (20 CFR 422.510).

**1** — Name of Beneficiary from Health Insurance Card
(Last) (First) (Middle)

**SEND COMPLETED FORM TO:**
Your Medicare Carrier
If you need help, call 1-800-MEDICARE
(1-800-633-4227)

**2** — Claim Number from Health Insurance Card

Patient's Sex
☐ Male
☐ Female

**3** — Patient's Mailing Address (City, State, Zip Code)
Check here if this is a new address ☐

_____
(Street or P.O. Box – Include Apartment Number)

_____
(City)   (State)   (Zip)

**3b** — Telephone Number
(Include Area Code)

( __ __ __ )

__ __ __ – __ __ __ __

**4** — Describe the illness or injury for which patient received treatment

**4b** Condition was related to:
A. Patient's employment
☐ Yes   ☐ No

B. Accident
☐ Auto   ☐ Other

**4c** Was patient being treated with chronic dialysis or kidney transplant?
☐ Yes   ☐ No

**5**
a. Are you employed and covered under an employee health plan?
☐ Yes   ☐ No

b. Is your spouse employed and are you covered under your spouse's employee health plan?
☐ Yes   ☐ No

c. If you have any medical coverage other than Medicare, such as private insurance, employment related insurance, State Agency (Medicaid), or the VA, complete:

Name and Address of other insurance, State Agency (Medicaid), or VA office

Policyholder's Name:

Policy or Medical Assistance No.

Note: If you DO NOT want payment information on this claim released, put an (X) here ☐

I AUTHORIZE ANY HOLDER OF MEDICAL OR OTHER INFORMATION ABOUT ME TO RELEASE TO THE SOCIAL SECURITY ADMINISTRATION AND CENTERS FOR MEDICARE & MEDICAID SERVICES OR ITS INTERMEDIARIES OR CARRIERS ANY INFORMATION NEEDED FOR THIS OR A RELATED MEDICARE CLAIM. I PERMIT A COPY OF THIS AUTHORIZATION TO BE USED IN PLACE OF THE ORIGINAL, AND REQUEST PAYMENT OF MEDICAL INSURANCE BENEFITS TO ME.

**6** — Signature of Patient (If patient is unable to sign, see Block 6 on reverse)

**6b** — Date signed

**IMPORTANT**
**ATTACH ITEMIZED BILLS FROM YOUR DOCTOR(S) OR SUPPLIER(S) TO THE BACK OF THIS FORM**

Form CMS-1490S (SC) (01/05)  EF 02/2005

# Form 19 College Application

## COMMON APPLICATION
## 2005–2006

### APPLICATION FOR UNDERGRADUATE ADMISSION

The member colleges and universities listed above fully support the use of this form. No distinction will be made between it and the college's own form. Please type or print in black ink.
Be sure to follow the instructions on the cover page of the Common Application booklet to complete, copy, and file your application with any one or several of the member colleges and universities.

### OPTIONAL DECLARATION OF EARLY DECISION/EARLY ACTION

Complete this section ONLY for the individual college to which you are applying ED or EA. It is your responsibility to follow that college's instructions regarding early admission, including obtaining and submitting any ED/EA form provided by that college. Do NOT complete this ED/EA section on copies of your application submitted to colleges for Regular Decision or Rolling Admission.

College Name _____ Deadline _____

☐ Early Decision    ☐ Early Action    ☐ EASC

## PERSONAL DATA

Legal Name _____
Enter name **exactly** as it appears on passports or other official documents.    Last/Family    First    Middle (complete)    Jr., etc.    Gender

Nickname (choose only one) _____    Former last name(s) if any _____

Are you applying as a ☐ freshman or ☐ transfer student?    For the term beginning _____

Birthdate ___ / ___ / ___    E-mail Address _____
mm/dd/yyyy

Permanent Home Address _____
Number and Street

_____
City or Town    State/Province    Country    Zip Code or Postal Code

Permanent Home Phone (_____) _____
Area Code    Number

*If different from above, please give your mailing address for all admission correspondence.*

Mailing Address (from ___ / ___ to ___ / ___) _____
(mm/yyyy)    (mm/yyyy)    Number and Street

_____
City or Town    State/Province    Country    Zip Code or Postal Code

Phone at mailing address (_____) _____    Cell phone (_____) _____
Area Code    Number    Area Code    Number

Citizenship ☐ US citizen    ☐ Dual US citizen; please specify other country of citizenship _____

☐ US Permanent Resident visa; citizen of _____    Alien Registration Number _____

☐ Other Citizenship _____    _____
Country(ies)    Visa type

If you are not a US citizen and live in the United States, how long have you been in the country? _____

Possible area(s) of academic concentration/major(s) _____    or undecided ☐

Special college or division if applicable _____

Possible career or professional plans _____    or undecided ☐
Will you be a candidate for financial aid? ☐ Yes ☐ No    If yes, the appropriate form(s) was/will be filed on _____

---

**The following items are optional. No information you provide will be used in a discriminatory manner.**

Place of birth _____    Social Security Number (if any) _____
City    State/Province    Country

First language, if other than English _____    Language spoken at home _____

If you wish to be identified with a particular ethnic group, please check all that apply

☐ African American, Black
☐ Native American, Alaska Native (tribal affiliation _____    enrolled _____)
☐ Asian American (countries of family's origin _____)
☐ Asian, including Indian Subcontinent (countries _____)
☐ Hispanic, Latino (countries _____)

☐ Mexican American, Chicano
☐ Native Hawaiian, Pacific Islander
☐ Puerto Rican
☐ White or Caucasian
☐ Other (specify _____)

2005–2006    AP-1

# Form 19 College Application

## EDUCATIONAL DATA

Secondary school you now attend (or from which you graduated) _____ Date of entry _____

Address _____ CEEB/ACT code _____
*Number and Street*

_____
*City or Town*     *State/Province*     *Country*     *Zip Code or Postal Code*

Date of secondary graduation _____ Type of school ☐ public ☐ private ☐ parochial ☐ home school

Guidance Counselor's Name _____ Counselor's E-mail _____

Position _____ Phone (____) _____ Fax (____) _____
                *Area Code*    *Number*    *Ext.*      *Area Code*     *Number*

List all other secondary schools, including summer schools and programs you have attended beginning with ninth grade.

| Name of School | Location (City, State/Province, Zip, Country) | Dates Attended |
|---|---|---|
| | | |
| | | |
| | | |

List all colleges/universities at which you have taken courses for credit; list names of courses taken and grades earned on a separate sheet. Please have an official transcript sent from each institution as soon as possible.

| Name of College/University & CEEB/ACT Code | Location (City, State/Province, Zip, Country) | Degree Candidate? | Dates Attended |
|---|---|---|---|
| | | ☐ | |
| | | ☐ | |
| | | ☐ | |

☐ Not currently attending school    ☐ Graduated from secondary school early.
Describe in detail, here or on a separate sheet, your activities since last enrolled.

If you are a resident of Alabama, Florida, Louisiana, Mississippi or Texas, are you currently displaced by Hurricane Katrina or Rita? If so, please take a moment to provide details of your displacement, here or on a separate sheet.

## TEST INFORMATION

Be sure to note the tests required for each institution to which you are applying. The official scores from the appropriate testing agency must be submitted to each institution as soon as possible. Please list your test plans below.

**ACT**

| Date taken/to be taken | English | Reading | Math | Science | Composite | Combination English/Writing |
|---|---|---|---|---|---|---|
| | | | | | | |
| | | | | | | |
| | | | | | | |

**SAT I or SAT Reasoning Tests**

| Date taken/to be taken | Verbal/Critical Reading | Math | Writing | Date taken/to be taken | Verbal/Critical Reading | Math | Writing | Date taken/to be taken | Verbal/Critical Reading | Math | Writing |
|---|---|---|---|---|---|---|---|---|---|---|---|
| | | | | | | | | | | | |

**SAT II or Subject Tests**

| Date taken/to be taken | Subject | Score | Date taken/to be taken | Subject | Score | Date taken/to be taken | Subject | Score |
|---|---|---|---|---|---|---|---|---|
| | | | | | | | | |
| | | | | | | | | |

**Test of English as a second language (TOEFL or other exam)**

| Test | Date taken/to be taken | Score | Test | Date taken/to be taken | Score |
|---|---|---|---|---|---|
| | | | | | |

AP-2                  2005–2006

# Form 19 College Application

## FAMILY

**Parent 1** _____

Last/Family     First     Middle     Gender

Living? ☐ Yes    ☐ No   (Date deceased _____ )

Home address if different from yours

_____

_____

Home phone _____

E-mail _____

Occupation _____

Name of employer _____

Work phone _____

Work e-mail _____

College (if any) _____

Degree _____ Year _____

Graduate school (if any) _____

Degree _____ Year _____

**Parent 2** _____

Last/Family     First     Middle     Gender

Living? ☐ Yes    ☐ No   (Date deceased _____ )

Home address if different from yours

_____

_____

Home phone _____

E-mail _____

Occupation _____

Name of employer _____

Work phone _____

Work e-mail _____

College (if any) _____

Degree _____ Year _____

Graduate school (if any) _____

Degree _____ Year _____

Parents' marital status:   ☐ married   ☐ separated   ☐ divorced (date _____ )   ☐ never married   ☐ widowed

With whom do you make your permanent home?   ☐ Parent 1   ☐ Parent 2   ☐ Both   ☐ Legal Guardian   ☐ Other relation

Legal guardian's name/address

Please give names and ages of your brothers or sisters. If they have attended college, give the names of the institutions attended, degrees, and approximate dates.

## EXTRACURRICULAR, PERSONAL, AND VOLUNTEER ACTIVITIES (including summer)

Please list your **principal** extracurricular, community, and family activities and hobbies **in the order of their interest to you.** Include specific events and/or major accomplishments such as musical instrument played, varsity letters earned, etc. Check ( ✓ ) in the right column those activities you hope to pursue in college. **To allow us to focus on the highlights of your activities, please complete this section even if you plan to attach a résumé.**

| Activity | Grade level or post-secondary (PS) 9 10 11 12 PS | Approximate time spent — Hours per week / Weeks per year | Positions held, honors won, or letters earned | Do you plan to participate in college? |
|---|---|---|---|---|
| _____ | ☐ ☐ ☐ ☐ ☐ | | _____ | ☐ |
| _____ | ☐ ☐ ☐ ☐ ☐ | | _____ | ☐ |
| _____ | ☐ ☐ ☐ ☐ ☐ | | _____ | ☐ |
| _____ | ☐ ☐ ☐ ☐ ☐ | | _____ | ☐ |
| _____ | ☐ ☐ ☐ ☐ ☐ | | _____ | ☐ |
| _____ | ☐ ☐ ☐ ☐ ☐ | | _____ | ☐ |
| _____ | ☐ ☐ ☐ ☐ ☐ | | _____ | ☐ |

## ACADEMIC HONORS

Briefly list or describe any scholastic distinctions or honors you have won since the ninth grade (e.g., National Merit, Cum Laude Society).

2005–2006

AP-3

# Form 19 College Application

## WORK EXPERIENCE

List any job (including summer employment) you have held during the past three years.

| Specific nature of work | Employer | Approximate dates of employment | Approximate no. of hours spent per week |
|---|---|---|---|
| | | | |
| | | | |
| | | | |
| | | | |

## SHORT ANSWER

Please describe which of your activities (extracurricular and personal activities or work experience) has been most meaningful and why (150 words or fewer).

## PERSONAL ESSAY

This personal statement helps us become acquainted with you in ways different from courses, grades, test scores, and other objective data. It will demonstrate your ability to organize thoughts and express yourself. We are looking for an essay that will help us know you better as a person and as a student. Please write an essay (250–500 words) on a topic of your choice or on one of the options listed below. *Please indicate your topic by checking the appropriate box below.*

☐ 1 Evaluate a significant experience, achievement, risk you have taken, or ethical dilemma you have faced and its impact on you.

☐ 2 Discuss some issue of personal, local, national, or international concern and its importance to you.

☐ 3 Indicate a person who has had a significant influence on you, and describe that influence.

☐ 4 Describe a character in fiction, an historical figure, or a creative work (as in art, music, science, etc.) that has had an influence on you, and explain that influence.

☐ 5 A range of academic interests, personal perspectives, and life experiences adds much to the educational mix. Given your personal background, describe an experience that illustrates what you would bring to the diversity in a college community, or an encounter that demonstrated the importance of diversity to you.

☐ 6 Topic of your choice.

☞ **Attach your essay on a separate sheet(s) (same size please). You <u>must</u> put your full name, date of birth, and name of secondary school <u>on each sheet</u>.**

**APPLICATION FEE PAYMENT**  ☐ Check/money order attached     ☐ Counselor-approved Fee Waiver attached

**REQUIRED SIGNATURE**  Your signature is required whether you are an ED, EA, EASC, or regular decision candidate.
*I certify that all information in my application, including my Personal Essay, is my own work, factually true, and honestly presented.*

Signature _____          Date _____

**IF APPLYING VIA EARLY DECISION OR EARLY ACTION**  (1) Complete the Optional ED/EA/EASC Declaration for your early application *only*. (2) Submit the college's required ED/EA/EASC form, if any. (3) Understand that it is your responsibility to report any changes in your schedule to the colleges to which you are applying.

These colleges are committed to administer all educational policies and activities without discrimination on the basis of race, color, religion, national or ethnic origin, age, handicap, or gender.

AP-4                                                                                                           2005–2006

# Form 20 Adopt-A-Highway Application

**ADOPT-A-HIGHWAY APPLICATION/PERMIT**
DT1206 398

Wisconsin Department of Transportation

Please complete this application and submit it to the appropriate Highway District Office. (See the map on "your Safety Comes First" Brochure) *Do not mail it to the WDOT Madison*

Group Name as it should appear on the sign (14 spaces on each of three lines.)
If you have more than 14, the letters will be smaller.

|  |  |  |  |  |  |  |  |  |  |  |  |  |  |
|--|--|--|--|--|--|--|--|--|--|--|--|--|--|
|  |  |  |  |  |  |  |  |  |  |  |  |  |  |
|  |  |  |  |  |  |  |  |  |  |  |  |  |  |
|  |  |  |  |  |  |  |  |  |  |  |  |  |  |

| Group Name | |
|---|---|
| Mailing Address | (Area Code) Facsimile Number |
| City, State, Zip Code | (Area Code) Telephone Number ñ Daytime |
| Contact Person Name | (Area Code) Telephone Number ñ Evening |
| Mailing Address | Approximate Number of People Participating in Each Cleanup |
| City, State, Zip Code | Number of Times Your Group Plans to Pick up Litter This Year ñ Minimum 3 Times |

Highway Section you Want to Adopt – List Alternate Sections in Order of Preference

| HIGHWAY NAME/NUMBER | FROM | TO | IN COUNTY |
|---|---|---|---|
|  |  |  |  |
|  |  |  |  |
|  |  |  |  |

By signature below, the Group acknowlledges the hazardous nature of the work and agrees to the terms can conditions stated on the back of this, or attached, form.

| Signature of Authorized Group Represenative ñ Must be 18 years or older | Date |
|---|---|
| Title | |

## DO NOT WRITE BELOW THIS LINE

**PERMIT APPROVAL** The Department approves this permit for the Group to participate in the Adopt-A-Highway Program for the section identified above. The Group accepts the responsibility of picking up litter on this section of highway. The Department reserves the right to modify or cancel this permit at any time. Please notify the District Adopt-A-Highway Coordinator with any Group information change.

| Adopt-A-Highway Coordinator Signature | Date | Permit Number |
|---|---|---|
|  |  |  |